A trail guide to walking

THE TWO MOORS WAY

from Lynmouth to Ivybridge

A Trail Guide to Walking the Two Moors Way:

From Lynmouth to Ivybridge

Copyright © Trail Wanderer Publications 2018
www.trailwanderer.co.uk
contact@trailwanderer.co.uk

First Printed 2018

Printed ISBN 978-1-9999509-0-3
Digital ISBN 978-1-9999509-3-4

Cover Photo – Stefanie Gross @stefgphoto
All other photographs - Matthew Arnold
Editor - Amber Mansfield
Designed by – Serena-June Horgan

Dedication

In memory of my grandfather Albert Bragg.
So your memory will live on.
1936 – 2016

TABLE OF CONTENTS

The Route

INTRODUCTION

I have lived in Devon all my life, however, as humans, we too often ignore those places closest to us in search of lands far away. As such, there were many areas local to me that I had never even thought of visiting. I certainly enjoy a challenge and the thought of walking the whole route of the Two Moors Way over the course of a few days while exploring more of my home county greatly appealed to me; trekking 100 miles living out of a backpack is no easy feat.

As much as I have a passion for adventure and discovery, I also have a desire to share my experiences in the hope that they will inspire and encourage you all to get out there and explore. This is ultimately why I decided to write this guidebook.

The Two Moors Way gives you a truly fantastic insight into the beauty of Devon, and a small part of Somerset, as the trail cuts from north to south. Owing to the alluring scenery you will see on your journey, it is easy to see why so many tourists are drawn to Devon each year. Starting at Lynmouth you will first see the spectacular cliffs rising high along the North Devon coast. You will then proceed onwards over the high moorland of Exmoor to descend into the very rural areas of North and Mid Devon. Travelling through farmsteads, rolling hills and passing through villages or small isolated hamlets, you will bypass the occasional thatched cob before finally entering onto Dartmoor. Thanks to the scattered rough outcrops of granite tors and prehistoric sites, Dartmoor is steeped in history and provides a wonderful finale.

The traditional route is from Ivybridge at the southern edge of Dartmoor to Lynmouth on the North Devon Coast. I decided to walk this route in the opposite direction, and this book will follow this route accordingly. I have broken the route into easily accomplishable legs and I hope this guide will serve you in venturing across and exploring the beauty of my home county, Devon.

THE TWO MOORS WAY AND THE HISTORY OF THE ROUTE.

Calls for a cross-county long-distance footpath in Devon date back to the 1960s. However, opposition by landowners meant any attempts to establish a new route were eventually struck down. Consequently, the Two Moors Way, the brainchild of Joseph Turner, head of the Two Moors Way Association, officially opened by Councillor Ted Pinney on the 29th May 1976 using existing rights of way. Today, it remains one of the oldest regional footpaths in Devon.

To summarise, the Two Moors Way is a long-distance footpath that stretches from Ivybridge in South Devon, to Lynmouth in the North. Its name comes from the two main areas adventurers pass through – both Dartmoor and Exmoor National Parks – the Two Moors. On route, the bustling town of Ivybridge soon gives way to the Dartmoor National Park and walkers venture across remote moorland high above the Erme Valley before crossing the Avon river and passing through Hameldown Beacon with its bronze age 'village'. Continuing on, visitors will pass Caste Drogo and through the tiny village of Drewsteington before venturing out of the moor and into mid-Devon. In mid- Devon, there is a range of beautiful quaint hamlets and villages to explore, from the likes of Hittisleigh to the more well-known village of Witheridge. Upon reaching West Anstey, the path begins to enter Exmoor National Park. Here, walkers will see some of the most remote areas of Exmoor and eventually pass into the county of Somerset. Albeit brief, after a few gorgeous miles, the path returns to Devon where it ultimately terminates at the seaside resort of Lynmouth. It is also possible to walk the route in reverse; as is the purpose of this guide.

Typically, the route is 103 miles (166km) long but this can vary due to weather conditions that sometimes render portions of the path inaccessible. The average fit person usually completes the route within a week, but of course, it is also possible to explore the area while taking your time to enjoy the history, scenery, and nature offered on the route. Though the walk is usually relatively easy, there a few exceptions that may provide challenges. Further, despite technological advancements, some sections require strong navigational skills think your traditional map and compass!

Over time, the route has slowly evolved. Though the Two Moors Way Association fell into disrepair after Joseph Turner's death in 2004, in 2016 the Association was reinvigorated to celebrate the fortieth anniversary of the route and to encourage more members of the public to undertake the challenge. The Association was given assistance by the National Lottery, Devon County Council, and both Dartmoor and Exmoor National Parks; the route now even has its own website **(www.twomoorsway.org)**.

ADDITIONAL ERME-PLYM TRAIL

Please note, the following is not covered in this book.

In 2005, the Erme-Plym Trail was combined with the Two Moors Way to establish a full Devon coast-to- coast route that spanned 115 miles. Though the precise date that the Erme-Plym Trail was initially established remains unknown, the trail links the beautiful seaside village of Wembury with the scenic Erme Valley, just south of Ivybridge, all located within the South Hams district. Adventurers choosing this route are taken through rolling pastoral panoramic scenes that span far beyond the eye's reach. Highlights of this section include passing through the small but historic village of Brixton, as well as the picturesque village of Yalmpton – home to the cottage that is rumoured to have been where the rhyme Old Mother Hubbard was written!

CHARACTERISTICS OF DEVON

EXMOOR & NORTH DEVON

Exmoor National Park, named after the River Exe, lies between the counties of Somerset and Devon in South West England. Spreading across 692.8km2, Exmoor is believed to have been occupied since the stone age but was not designated a National Park until 1954. This past year, there were approximately 1.4 million visitor days.

The area is generally composed of deep valleys and hilly open moorland, but Exmoor also boasts 55km (34m) of the Bristol Channel coastline with soaring cliffs to match. Moorland accounts for a quarter of the Exmoor Park and differs from other UK moors as it is wetter and milder, consequently allowing a longer growing season and more livestock. For those hikers among you, the highest point in Exmoor at a modest 519m is Dunkery Hill. For a more leisurely stroll, the Brendon Hills offers a wonderful alternative as the terrain is broken by a number of rivers and streams that caress the curves of the landscape. Speaking of landscapes, any budding geologists are bound to encounter old and new red sandstone, shales, limestone, and Devonian slates. Finally, Exmoor is home to widespread oak woodland. With over 9,000 hectare acres, the woods in Exmoor were formerly designated a royal forest and preserved for hunting purposes. Today, the area is host to a variety of wildlife and fun activities for all to enjoy.

The main settlements in the area include Lynton and Lynmouth, Dulverton, Porlock, and Dunster, but there are several smaller cosy villages, hamlets, and farms that litter the landscape. In Simonsbath, for example, you can find an Iron Age hillfort and the remains of Wheal Eliza mine. You can also find other examples of impressive architecture, the Tarr Steps, for instance, is home to an ancient clapper bridge, the longest of its type in the whole of the UK. Near to Porlock, there is also an ancient stone circle; while the purpose of it is unknown, it one of only two stone circles to survive in this area. Finally, Exmoor is rich in archaeologically discoveries as it is home to nearly 400 prehistoric burial mounds.

MID DEVON

The Mid-Devon section of the Two Moors Way is far gentler than the two Moors National Parks. Winding country roads, bridleways, and ancient footpaths link settlements and farms en route. Overall, the pastoral landscape, endless meadows, and calm rolling hills create a scene that is undeniably and quintessentially British. It should be noted that compared to the national parks, there are very little facilities along this part of the route, especially in terms of shops for supplies, so be sure to stock up before you head out. This section makes for a far more leisurely stroll than the hardships one may face at Exmoor or Dartmoor, so enjoy it, take your time, and explore all the countryside has to offer.

DARTMOOR

Dartmoor National Park, named after the River Dart running through it, lies entirely in the county of Devon. Set between Plymouth and Exeter, Dartmoor was granted National Park status in 1951; it consequently became a protected area. Prehistoric remains on Dartmoor date back to the Neolithic period, and the area itself contains the largest the largest concentration of Bronze Age remains in the UK.

Dartmoor is steeped in interesting legends, myths, and folklore. Pixies, witchcraft, ghosts, headless horseman, and weird on-goings are rumoured to frequent the landscape. In 1638, rumour even has it that a Great Thunderstorm led the Devil to visit the moorland village of Widecombe-in- the-Moor. Undoubtedly, the thick mist, remoteness, and dark nights contribute to this popular image as the expansive moorland can, at times, appear bleak and desolate. As a result, this haunting scenery has seen Dartmoor inspire a plethora of writers and films. Sir Arthur Conan Doyle's The Hound of the Baskervilles is set in the grounds of Dartmoor, as is James Hewitt's Love and War. When it comes to films, Dartmoor has provided the backdrop for hit movies such as Steven Spielberg's War Horse (2011), and Stephen Frear's Tamara Drewe (2010).

Dartmoor is also home to a training area used by the British army since 1800. After a major prison opened in the area in 1809, soldiers guarding the prison began practising in the area. Over time, troops were drawn to the area owing to the diverse landscape. Today, military training is still carried out by the

Navy, Marines, Army and Air Force. Two training camps are located here, and three firing ranges.

It is important to highlight that Dartmoor National Park is the only park in England that allows visitors to wild camp. If you are backpack camping, then the official Dartmoor website states that it is acceptable to do so for one or two nights in some areas of open moorland so long as you stay well away from settlements or roads, and utilise a 'no impact' approach. Please note, preparation and planning are essential in this case as this sort of camping, despite popular belief, is not actually permitted in all areas of Dartmoor.

When it comes to the landscape itself, covering 954km, Dartmoor is graced with a variety of rivers, bogs, moorland, and hills. Locals often refer to the area as 'The Great Swamp' owing to the erratic nature of the terrain. The highest point, at 621 metres, is the High Willhays and it is, in fact, the highest point in the south of England. For those with an interest in geology, Dartmoor has the largest area of granite in Britain (625 km2). There are also many tors in Dartmoor; these are outcrops of rocks that are the remains of volcanic activity thousands of years ago. There are in fact over 160 hills in Dartmoor with the word tor in their name. Finally, the hilly and often stupendous looking landscape means the park is home to an abundance of walking and cycling routes, suitable for varying levels of fitness.

WILDLIFE & VEGETATION

WILDLIFE

The Two Moors Way is home to a fantastic array of rare and beautiful animals. Dartmoor, for example, is home to over fifty percent of Britain's population of several globally threatened species. In Devon more widely you can find wonderful birds, butterflies, deer, otters, and horses – to name a few. The moors are particularly renowned for their butterflies, moths, bees, wasps, dragonflies, and damselflies. The 'All The Moor Butterflies' project has helped to create and restore habitat for several endangered butterflies, from the Pearl-bordered Fritillary to the High Brown Fritillary and the Marsh fritillary; consequently, there are several rare creatures that you may be lucky enough to see for the first time.

There are also many horses on this route that make for an iconic sight on the moors. The Exmoor and Dartmoor ponies are native breeds to the British Isles, and, if you are lucky, you may see some roaming around - many are semi-feral livestock today. Exmoor ponies are considered endangered, and their existence is threatened. Similarly, there are only thought to be around 1,500 remaining Dartmoor ponies in the national park. Written record of the Dartmoor ponies' dates back to 1012 AD; they have had many practical use over time, especially when transporting granite from the quarry, but today they are more of a cultural landmark and by grazing on the land they help to maintain surrounding habitats and support nearby wildlife.

Other mammals to spot include the famous red deer, a species that has survived on Exmoor since the pre-historic era. Once hunted by the King when the area was designated a royal forest, today it is possible to see calves being born in the months of June and July by the edge of the woodland, or near to the moorland vegetation. Alternatively, if you are very lucky, you might be able to spot an otter in Dartmoor. Once commonplace, a serious decline in the number has led to extreme conservation efforts to enable a comeback. As part of the effort to raise awareness of their demise, you can actually follow an otter trail around the National Park.

EXMOOR HAS ONE OF THE HIGHEST
TICK POPULATIONS IN THE UK

While the wildlife is beautiful, one thing to watch out for on this walk are ticks; these little insects can carry diseases and the infection rate in any place varies from 0 to 15%. Though they are most active between March and October, they can still strike even on mild winter days. As they are very small, ticks often go unnoticed, and since you are unlikely to feel the tick attach itself to your body, you should periodically and thoroughly check your skin; the bites can be as small as a poppy seed. Exercise caution when removing a tick as you need to ensure you remove all parts of its body. You can buy tick removal tools online, or if you lack tools use pointed tweezers or fine thread, so long as they are cleaned thoroughly with antiseptic. If you begin to experience symptoms of Lyme disease – extreme tiredness, muscle weakness, headaches, upset digestive system, muscle pain etc. please seek medical advice immediately.

VEGETATION

When it comes to nature in Exmoor, the national park is fortunate to be the home of a number of rare trees, including the exclusive home of whitebeam trees. There are also several ancient trees, in fact, compared to the rest of the world Exmoor has a significant population of such trees. Dartmoor, meanwhile, has weather that classifies their woodlands as temperate rainforests. Consequently, mature oak trees are covered in various lichens, mosses, and ferns that often can only grow in this area because of its conditions.

In Emsworthy, located in Dartmoor National Park, part of the 'high' moor, visitors in the months of May and June can witness the fields bursting with colour owing to the abundance of bluebells that grow in the region. Further, exploring the forested areas of Dartmoor, such as the Dunsford Woods, will reveal a plethora of daffodils painting the landscape with glowing shades of yellow. Overall, a large portion of granite, heavy rainfall, and acidic soil has meant a unique variety of plants have grown and adapted to these harsh conditions.

WEATHER

Editor's note: The passage below was calculated using statistics gathered by the met office based on historical data for the period 1981-2010.

Please note, the weather on Dartmoor can be unpredictable even at the best of times. Using Yarner Wood as an example, in the winter, the average daytime temperature ranges from a mere 2° c to a similarly cold 5 °c. In the summer, temperatures range from roughly 10° c to 22° c. When it comes to rain, Dartmoor has an average yearly total of 1384mm. By far, the wettest months are October through to February, with an average of 155mm per month. From March to September, these months' average just 100mm per month. Note, July has the least rain with only 70mm on average. On average, there are 152 days of the year that have greater than, or equal to, 1mm of rainfall. That leaves 213 days with no rainfall at all. The winter months' average of 14 days of precipitation per month, and there are approximately 8 days a month in the summer. This is just one area of Dartmoor, however, and it is important in Dartmoor to be prepared for all types of weather, from sudden thunderstorms and heavy downpour to extreme mist, fog, and even snow.

In mid-Devon, taking North Wyke as an example, the average yearly maximum temperature is 13.4° c. In the summer months, average maximum temperature ranges from 17 to 20° c, while minimum temperature ranges from 10 to 12° c. In the winter months, average maximum temperature ranges from 7 to 10° c while minimum temperatures range from 2 to 5° c. There is a yearly average of 1053.3mm rainfall in this region. Winter months average 114mm of rainfall, while summer months average 62mm per month. Matching the weather at Dartmoor, overall, on average there are 152 days per year where there is more than, or equal to, 1mm of rainfall. Again, leaving 213 days with no rainfall at all.

Exmoor's weather, based on the climate station in Liscombe, an area on the Two Moors Way, has a yearly average maximum temperature of 12° c, while the average minimum temperature is 5.8° c. In the summer months, average daytime maximum temperature lies between 15 and 19° c, while the average minimum temperature ranges between 7 and 10° c. In the winter months, average daytime maximum temperature lies between 5 and 9° c, while the average minimum temperature ranges between 1 and 5° c. When it comes to rainfall, on average the area has a yearly total of 1145.2mm of rainfall. The wettest months are from November to January, averaging 163mm per month. The driest months are from April to July, averaging just 86mm a month. The other months lie between these two. On average, there are 174 days of the year that have greater than, or equal to, 1mm of rainfall. That leaves 191 days with no rainfall at all. When it comes to wind at 10m, the yearly average is 9.6kn. November to April have average speeds of 10.98kn per month, while May to October has speeds on average of 8.1kn per month.

Overall weather forecasts are crucial and hourly weather watching is a key skill required to navigate this route especially over the open moorland. Looking out for wind direction and the appearance of clouds will enable you to determine how to best prepare for the remainder of your walk. Ensure you take this advice into consideration when packing your bag as it is important to carry the correct kit.

PREPARATION

ACCOMMODATION

Along the Two Moors Way, there is a multitude of quaint hotels and numerous bed and breakfasts to suit all tastes. In fact, there are so many that it is an impossible task to give credit to all of those on the route. As such, at the beginning of each section, selected accommodation will be mentioned but it is advisable to spend some time on your own researching in advance suitable stopover locations.

Alternatively, if you decide to camp on this route, there are a plethora of campsites to choose from. However, it should be noted that these are often located away from the main trail. Consequently, you should remember to account for the added distance it may take should you wish to stop somewhere off-route.

The final option is sleeping wild. Please remember that all land in England and Wales is owned and so you would need to seek permission of the landowner before bivvying or pitching up. The only exception is on Dartmoor National Park. Again, however, as briefly touched upon in the introduction, you have to be located at least one hundred metres from the road, and you cannot be visible from nearby dwellings, or the road itself. Further, visitors are asked to avoid archaeological sites, farmland, and moorland that is surrounded by walls and floodplains. Overall, be sure to check the Wild Camping Map provided by Dartmoor National Park to ensure you are abiding by all of the rules **(www.trailwanderer.co.uk/information/dartmoor-wild-camping-map.pdf).**

FOOD AND NUTRITION

When it comes to food and nutrition while walking the Two Moors Way, it is vital to ensure you plan for the entire length of your trip to guarantee you have enough calories to sustain yourself. This should involve looking at each leg of your walk and considering what food you need that day to help you complete the distance required. This is one of the fun parts of preparing for the walk as it gives you a chance to be creative, consider what food goes well together, and perhaps even trying things you have not eaten before. You should also consider taking vitamins to supplement any lack of nutrients. It is a good idea to separate your food into days so you know exactly what you are having on each and do not run out of food faster than expected. If you have allowed yourself extra days for a detour, be sure to account for the energy needed to complete these sections too.

When it comes to backpack size, food and water will make up the main bulk of your pack weight. Remember that one litre of water weighs one kilogram so this is going to substantially add a great deal of weight to your overall pack. In some parts, the path can become arduous with steep or be it short hills so you are likely to break a sweat. As your body uses water to regulate an optimum working temperature, water should not be skimped on!

In order to ensure the lowest weight possible, dispose of all food packaging before you depart. This will also rid you of all the litter you would then have to carry around as this is just dead weight. You should also aim to pack light-weight food that is easy to prepare as it will require fewer utensils to do so. If you are worried about a lack of flavour, it may be a good idea to carry small sachets of spices to make meals more exciting.

Snacks: When it comes to snacks to eat on-the- go, cereal and muesli bars are great options. It is also nice to make your own trail mix. Simply purchase a bag of your favourite nuts, seeds, chocolate chips, and dried fruit and then place them into a small bag to keep on yourself for easy access and energy along the way. All of these can also be eaten separately depending on what resources you have, or that you can find along the way. Other options include rice cakes, chocolate bars, whole-grain tortillas, energy bars, chews or gels.

Main Meals: For main meals, you want to be taking on a good mixture of complex and simple carbohydrates. For breakfast, I would advise porridge oats or wheat flakes, with a bit of powdered milk mixed separately, even topped with some dried fruit. For dinner, noodles, pasta, and rice make safe, cheap, and light options - though rice can take a lot longer to cook. While dehydrated meals and boil in the bags are handy, they are often expensive and use both a lot of fuel and a lot of water. Of course, do not forget to pack instant coffee and tea sachets to make a refreshing cuppa.

VILLAGE PUBS, SHOPS AND CAFES

Along the route, you will pass through many villages. These areas offer a variety of local amenities such as pubs, cafes, and village shops where they will serve decent local produce. Here you can stock up on supplies, or just enjoy a hearty meal in one of the pubs. At the start of each upcoming section, these facilities will be listed, so make sure you account for the time spent in each place as well as the opening and closing time of aforementioned establishments.

The Church House Inn, Holne

NAVIGATION

When passing through the farmland, along hedgerows, over fields and through woodland, the path is well trodden and quite distinctly visible as well as very clearly waymarked. There are areas though, most notably over the long stretches of moorland within Exmoor and Dartmoor, that provide exceptions to this statement. Here you will find very little in the way of directions as signs are virtually non-existent. You should also bear in mind that although the authorities responsible for maintaining the trail do a great job with the upkeep and repair of signs, they are always going to be vulnerable and succumb to the elements and nature. Maps, therefore, are absolutely essential.

Below this paragraph, I have included the detailed maps that cover each leg of the route that you can purchase if you wish. Please note, only a very small section of the route appears on OS Explorer 127. With that said, I would suggest that rather than carrying all of these maps (taking up valuable space and weight), a better alternative would be to print off the sections you need. I recommend opting for the 1:25 000 maps as it will give you a greater detail of the terrain. You can do this by visiting the ordnance survey website at **(https://osmaps.ordnancesurvey.co.uk)**. You will need to take out a premium subscription to access the OS Leisure maps but you will be thanking me when you remember how much weight you are saving!

MAPS COVERING THE ROUTE

OS Explorer Maps
1:25 000 scale
4cm = 1km

Exmoor,
Explorer OL9
Barnstaple, Lynton, Minehead & Dulverton

South Molton & Chumleigh
Explorer 127
King's Nympton, Chittlehampton & Dolton

Okehampton,
Explorer 113
Hatherleigh, North Tawton & Lapford

Exeter & The Exe Valley,
Explorer 114
Crediton, Tiverton & Dulverton

Dartmoor,
Explorer OL28
Dartmoor

OS Landranger Maps
1:50 000 scale
2cm = 1km

Landranger 180
Barnstaple & Ifracombe

Minehead & Landranger 181
Minehead & Brendon Hills

Landranger 191
Okehampton & North Dartmoor

Landranger 202
Torbay & South Dartmoor

SIGNPOSTS & WAYMARKERS

Along the route you will find numerous different types of waymarkers and signs dotted along the trail to help guide the way. Be sure to keep an eye out for them! Below are some of the examples that you will encounter:

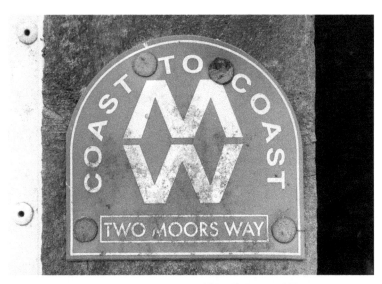

KIT LIST

As with any expedition, planning is an absolute requirement and compiling a suitable kit list of essential items to take with you is fundamental. Narrowing down the essential items that you need will ensure that you have a happier and safe experience. Depending on the type of outing that you have in mind, whether it be a country ramble, a backpacking holiday, or scaling the largest mountain ranges in the world, you are going to have to create a kit list specific to your expedition.

With the Two Moors Way lasting around 103 miles, you need to consider whether you are going to complete the trail in small sections or a continuous number of days. Below is a general kit list that will give you some idea of the equipment that you might want to consider. This is the kit that I carried on my trip for 5 days but you can tailor it to your needs. You can print this kit list out by visiting **(www.trailwanderer.co.uk/information/kit-list.pdf)**

Item	Notes	✓
Walking Boots		
Walking Trousers		
Top	Moisture wicking top	
Coat	Sufficient enough for wet and windy weather	
£50 / Wallet	Ensure enough cash should you require transport or supplies	
Keys		
Map + Map Cover		
Compass / GPS		
Matches / Lighter		
Note Book & Pen	To keep a journal or to keep a note of accommodation on the route	
Watch	Smart watch to log the route	
Beanie Hat		
Buff		
Head Torch		
Compass		

PERSONAL KIT CARRIED IN PACK

Item	Notes	✓
Waterproof Liner	To line the inside of the pack	
Sleeping Bag		
Bivvy Bag		
Roll Mat		
Warm Kit	Softie down jacket	
Spare socks	4 Pairs	
Spare underwear	4 Pairs	
Towel	Antibacterial towel	
Jet Boil / Cooking system	Spare gas	
Hoochie / Tent	Tent pegs	
Bungees	5	
Hydration pack	2 litre	
Spare Water	2 litre	
First aid Kit	Plasters, deep heat, anti-fungal powder	
Food / Emergency Rations	Noodles, boil in the bags, trail mix, nutrition bars	
Lighter/matches	For lighting cooker	
Gloves		
Hand Wipes	Antibacterial wipes	
Survival Blanket		
Rubbish Bag	For food packaging/general rubbish	

ADDITIONAL KIT

Item	Notes	✓
Spare batteries	3x AAA	
Spare Laces		
Flip Flops / Light weight trainers		
Portable charger	Charging phone/head torch	
Sun glasses		
Thermal Mug		
Brew Kit	Coffee sachets	
Multi tool		
Walking poles		

GETTING TO THE START POINT (LYNMOUTH)

BY RAIL AND BUS/TAXI VIA BARNSTAPLE

The Tarka line runs seven days a week and has connected North and South Devon since the mid-1800s. It is the main rail line that runs between Exeter and Barnstaple and is noted as being one of Britain's most scenic railway journeys. The line follows the River Creedy, River Yeo and River Taw. The commute is roughly an hour depending on the number of stops requested.

Unfortunately, there are no rail services that take you directly into Lynmouth. However, you can still travel by rail to Barnstaple station then transfer via local bus services or a taxi. If you choose to travel by bus, then upon arrival at Barnstaple train station there is a short walk to get you warmed up (approximately 0.6mi) to the main bus station. Head towards the River Taw and cross over Long Bridge, and follow the A3125 around to the right until you see the bus station over on your left.

The bus that provides the onward trip into Lynmouth is the 309/310 operated by Fliers and runs through the week from Monday through to Saturday with the first bus departing at 08:05 am. Please note, this was correct at the time of publication but for the latest up-to- date information please check **(www.filers.co.uk/bus.htm)**

If you're keen to get to Lynmouth and set off as soon as possible, or want to preserve your energy, then a taxi from Barnstaple might be more suitable. There are a number of taxi ranks that operate 24hrs a day to be found around Barnstaple city centre, with the closest being located outside the front of the railway station. A selected list of taxi numbers for Barnstaple can be found under Useful Information on page 110

BY CAR

Unless you plan on getting dropped off at the start point, you will need to seriously consider if you would be happy to leave your car in one spot for so long. More importantly, you also need to consider how you are going to make it back to the start point to pick up your car once you have completed the trail.

Though Lynmouth & Lynton provide numerous car parking facilities, it is advisable to arrive early in peak season as it turns into a tourist hotspot since people flock to the surrounding beauty and charm of the location. More information on car parking location and fees can be found by visiting **(www.visitlyntonandlynmouth.com/visit/carparks).**

The fastest route, whether you will be travelling from the north, east or south, is to come off at **junction 27** on the **M5**, signposted Tiverton. You should join the **A361** (North Devon Link Road) and follow signs towards Barnstaple for approximately 25 miles until you come to a roundabout with Lynton signposted. Here, take the fourth exit as you join onto the **A399** and continue along for another 12 miles before turning right onto the **A39**. Continue along the **A39** until you reach Barbrook Filling station and take the fork left directly opposite onto the **B3234** – this will lead all the way down into Lynmouth.

LEAVING THE FINISH POINT (IVYBRIDGE)

BY RAIL

Leaving Ivybridge is a lot easier than getting to the start point. Although it is a bit of a walk from the town centre, you will find the railway station located on the outskirts to the northeast of Ivybridge. This train line is part of the South Devon Main Line and passes between London Paddington and Penzance; trains serve the station every 2 hours. Note, there are no station facilities apart from a few benches. Unless you have pre-booked tickets you will need to purchase them from the conductor on board as there are also no ticket machines. If you require cash, the closest cash machines can be found in the town centre.

BY BUS

If you find that a bus would be more convenient in getting home. You have three main bus routes in Ivybridge that either depart from the town or pass through it. The longest of these routes, the X38, runs between Exeter and Plymouth and passes through Ivybridge; the main stop is located outside the town hall. Alternatively, the Gold route runs between Torquay and Plymouth, once again passing through Ivybridge and stopping at the town hall. Finally, the 20A bus runs between Ivybridge and Plymouth. All the above routes are provided by Stagecoach and operate Monday through to Saturday except on public holidays. Again, please visit **(www.stagecoachbus.com/plan-a- journey)** for up to date information.

MILEAGE CHART

Two Moors Way	km	miles	Elevation Gain
Lynmouth – Simonsbath	16	9.5	608m
Simonsbath – Withypool	10	6.2	137m
Withypool – Hawkridge	9.5	5.9	143m
Hawkridge – Knowstone	10	6.2	279m
Knowstone – Witheridge	12	7.5	172m
Witheridge – Morchard Bishop	11.5	7.1	196m
Morchard Bishop – Drewsteignton	24.5	15.2	569m
Drewsteignton – Widecombe-in- the-moor	25	15.5	634m
Widecombe-in- the-moor – Holne	11	7	346m
Holne – Ivybridge	21.5	13	449m

The mileage chart, pictured above, is used to indicate the distance between each of the major villages on route. As well as this, the mileage chart shows the expected elevation gain within each leg of the walk. As you can see, leg 7, 8, and 10 are the longest sections of the walk. Leg 7, from Morchard Bishop to Drewsteignton, is along the mid-Devon part of the route and it is here that you will follow several hedgerows and pass through multiple farms. Leg 8 and 10, however, are long stretches across open moorland of Dartmoor National Park.

Please note: All figures given are approximations, these distances and elevation gains will vary based on diversions.

LEG 1 – LYNMOUTH TO SIMONSBATH

Lynmouth

OS Grid Ref: SS 7309 5011
District: North Devon
OS Explorer map: OL9: Exmoor

Distance: 16km / 9.5miles
Elevation Gain: 608m

Points of Interests
- Public toilets
- Public Car Parks
- Lynmouth Flood Memorial Hall
- Cliff Railway

Accommodation and eateries
- Esplanade Fish Bar
- Riverside Restaurant
- The Rising Sun
- Fish On The Harbour
- The Village Inn
- Lynmouth Bay Café
- Coffee Mill
- The Ancient Mariner
- The Bake House café and Takeaway
- The Pavilion Dining Room

Buses
Filers Travel 309 / 310,
Barnstaple – Lynton/Lynmouth
(Monday to Saturday)

The small village of Lynmouth, twinned with Lynton, straddles East and West Lyn rivers. Lynmouth is therefore located in a gorge, seven-hundred feet below the town of Lynton. Together, only approximately 1,647 people live in Lynton and Lynmouth. The two areas are connected via a breath-taking trip on the Cliff Railway; a cable car powered by water tanks and good old gravity. Lynmouth itself lies both on the coast, and by the northern edge of Exmoor National Park. If it takes your fancy, the Sillery Sands beach, located nearby, is frequented by naturists from all over the country. However, if art is more your scene, then the English landscape and portrait painter, Thomas Gainsborough, famously stated that Lynmouth is "the most delightful place for a landscape painter this country can boast."

As beautiful as Lynmouth and the surrounding area is, it would be wise to not hang around for too long. Ideally, you should want to set off early in the morning. You will be pleased to know that whatever way you go to get out of Lynmouth, the only way is up! So with that in mind let's set off.

A From Lynmouth's old harbour lighthouse head along Riverside Road leading away from the Harbour passing all the shops on your right, until you reach the junction and bridge on your left. Turn right, then take the very first left onto Watersmeet Road. Cross over to the right-hand side where the path leads up a slight incline and follow it around to the right. **B** Upon reaching the first lamppost, take a right up the lane leading uphill in between the houses.

If you are not used to hills or carrying a heavy backpack, then the next few hundred metres are going to be tough. It is an approximately 1km walk along winding paths and through the densely wooded hillside to get to the top, with an elevation gain of 200m. **C** However, when you reach the top of Oxen Tor you will be rewarded with a spectacular view of Lynmouth peeking through the trees: an idyllic photo opportunity. A little further past Oxen Tor as you head out of the woodland, follow the ridgeline along for a short distance. The path then starts to descend slightly until it again rises to just below the ridgeline of the hill on your right. Along this stretch you will come across a few benches, these are great for taking frequent rests to recover from the initial uphill slog. The path eventually swoops around to the right again sticking to the contour of the hill before passing through an old settlement which has since long vanished. Eventually, the path starts to lead downhill and comes out onto the bend of Shamble Way (a section of the A39). **D** Upon joining the road, head down towards the junction and take the first right before the bridge then head on through into Combe Park Wood National

View from Oxen Tor

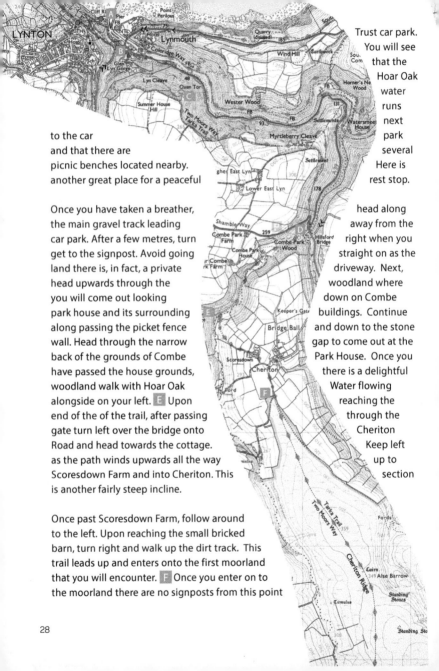

Trust car park. You will see that the Hoar Oak water runs next park several Here is rest stop.

to the car and that there are picnic benches located nearby. another great place for a peaceful

Once you have taken a breather, the main gravel track leading car park. After a few metres, turn get to the signpost. Avoid going land there is, in fact, a private head upwards through the you will come out looking park house and its surrounding along passing the picket fence wall. Head through the narrow back of the grounds of Combe have passed the house grounds, woodland walk with Hoar Oak alongside on your left. E Upon end of the of the trail, after passing gate turn left over the bridge onto Road and head towards the cottage. as the path winds upwards all the way Scoresdown Farm and into Cheriton. This is another fairly steep incline.

head along away from the right when you straight on as the driveway. Next, woodland where down on Combe buildings. Continue and down to the stone gap to come out at the Park House. Once you there is a delightful Water flowing reaching the through the Cheriton Keep left up to section

Once past Scoresdown Farm, follow around to the left. Upon reaching the small bricked barn, turn right and walk up the dirt track. This trail leads up and enters onto the first moorland that you will encounter. F Once you enter on to the moorland there are no signposts from this point

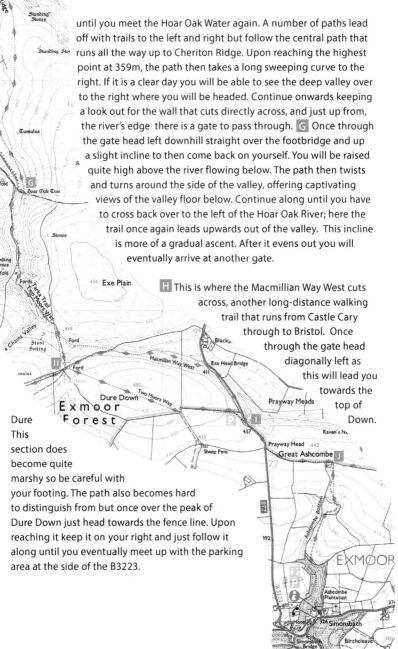

until you meet the Hoar Oak Water again. A number of paths lead off with trails to the left and right but follow the central path that runs all the way up to Cheriton Ridge. Upon reaching the highest point at 359m, the path then takes a long sweeping curve to the right. If it is a clear day you will be able to see the deep valley over to the right where you will be headed. Continue onwards keeping a look out for the wall that cuts directly across, and just up from, the river's edge there is a gate to pass through. **G** Once through the gate head left downhill straight over the footbridge and up a slight incline to then come back on yourself. You will be raised quite high above the river flowing below. The path then twists and turns around the side of the valley, offering captivating views of the valley floor below. Continue along until you have to cross back over to the left of the Hoar Oak River; here the trail once again leads upwards out of the valley. This incline is more of a gradual ascent. After it evens out you will eventually arrive at another gate.

H This is where the Macmillian Way West cuts across, another long-distance walking trail that runs from Castle Cary through to Bristol. Once through the gate head diagonally left as this will lead you towards the top of Down.

Dure
This section does become quite marshy so be careful with your footing. The path also becomes hard to distinguish from but once over the peak of Dure Down just head towards the fence line. Upon reaching it keep it on your right and just follow it along until you eventually meet up with the parking area at the side of the B3223.

From the car park, head right along the B3223, keeping to the left verge for a few metres until you come across a small layby. Enter through the gate on your left and into the field just before the layby. Once through, keep close to the hedge line until you reach the sign directing you right.

Next, navigate your way through the marshland. There are a few footbridges to aid you but this is another section to be wary about if you do not want to get wet feet! Once you have tackled the marsh, head towards the dense patch of woodland and follow the tree line around and down into the public car park situated at the top of Simonsbath.

Near to Hoar Oak Tree

The base of Dure Down

LEG 2 – SIMONSBATH TO WITHYPOOL

Simonsbath

OS Grid Ref: SS 7744 3933
District: West Somerset
OS Explorer map: OL9: Exmoor

Distance: 10km / 6.2 miles
Elevation Gain: 137m

Points of Interests
- Public Car Park
- Public Toilets
- St Luke's Church
- Medieval Bridge
- Simonsbath Saw Mill

Accommodation and eateries
- The Exmoor Forest Inn
- Simonsbath House Hotel & Cottages

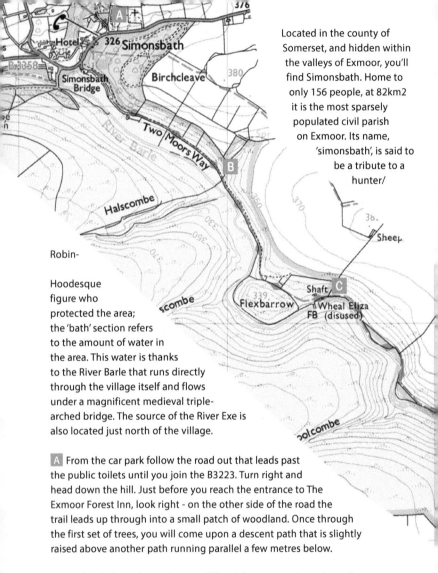

Located in the county of Somerset, and hidden within the valleys of Exmoor, you'll find Simonsbath. Home to only 156 people, at 82km2 it is the most sparsely populated civil parish on Exmoor. Its name, 'simonsbath', is said to be a tribute to a hunter/

Robin-

Hoodesque figure who protected the area; the 'bath' section refers to the amount of water in the area. This water is thanks to the River Barle that runs directly through the village itself and flows under a magnificent medieval triple-arched bridge. The source of the River Exe is also located just north of the village.

A From the car park follow the road out that leads past the public toilets until you join the B3223. Turn right and head down the hill. Just before you reach the entrance to The Exmoor Forest Inn, look right - on the other side of the road the trail leads up through into a small patch of woodland. Once through the first set of trees, you will come upon a descent path that is slightly raised above another path running parallel a few metres below.

As you head along this path, you will be able to sneak views through the trees at the towering moorland hills over to your right; the River Barle running at its base.

B Eventually, you will pass through a gate where you will then leave the shelter of the trees behind. The path gradually leads downhill until you are nearly level with the river before it starts to rise again. In the distance, you will see that the River Barle curves away round to the right while the path leads up to the large mound that is Flex barrow. **C** As you walk around Flex Barrow you'll happen upon the disused Wheal Eliza mine, an unsuccessful Copper mine dating back to the mid-nineteenth century. There are also stone ruins of the mine works that are still visible.

Wheal Eliza Mine

Wheal Eliza was active around the mid-1800s. It consisted of several shafts reaching a depth of 300 feet. It first worked as a copper mine and later turned into an iron mine, both of which eventually failed to mine any ore. After these unsuccessful attempts the mine was abandoned and flooded.

The mine also holds a gruesome history. In 1858, a seven-year-old girl by the name of Anna Burgess was killed by her drunken father. After months of searching, it was only when the local magistrates ordered the abandoned mine to be drained that a bag containing the child's body was eventually found. Her father later admitted to killing her and was sent to the gallows in Taunton on the 4th January 1859.

As you continue onwards, the path eventually joins back up with the River Barle. Veering left through a meadow, you should shortly join a grassy track. This next section can become extremely boggy. From here though, you should just be able to see Cow Castle in the distance. Formerly an Iron Age hill fort, it is also a scheduled monument.

D When you reach Cow Castle I recommend a climb to the top as the views looking back down the valley from where you have just walked are

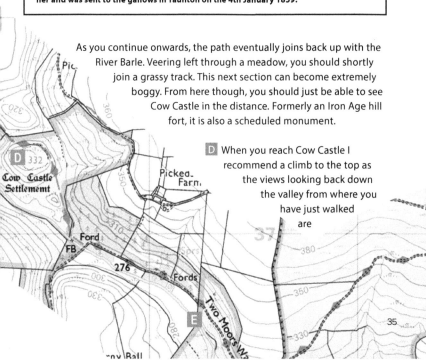

35

Please Shut Gate

Near to Flex Barrow

Kitridge Lane

quite stunning. It also gives you a great insight into the direction of where you are headed next.

A short distance on from Cow Castle, enter through the gate into once what would have been a large area of woodland. Today it has sadly succumbed to deforestation with no signs of any tees being replanted. What once would have been a beautiful woodland walk has now been turned into a graveyard of tree stumps. Head straight through the area ensuring you keep the River Barle on your right-hand side.

Next, pass through another gate and this will take you to the north-west section of Withypool Common. E You will now be on moorland again so expect the terrain to be very muddy and boggy. The trail then takes a large

sweep around to the left and an incline brings you to the summit of the hill. It may seem like a bit of a slog, however, the views towards the east are well worth the effort as you can see the River Barle snaking off in the distance towards Withypool. You may even catch a glimpse of Landacre Bridge in the distance. This is another monument that is thought to date back to the medieval period. Once you made it up and come level with a barn at the top the trail morphs into a more solid dirt track. Head down the track until you hit Landacre Lane. **F** Continue straight over and through the gate onto Kitridge Lane.

> **Cow Castle**
>
> Fortified refuges such as hill forts first appeared in the late Bronze and early Iron Age. Cow Castle is one such example occupying a hilltop within the valley of The River Barle. It is well worth the climb to the top to see the striking views.

As you continue along the lane you will catch glimpses through the trees on your right of Brightworthy Barrows and Withypool Hill. Set amongst Withypool Common, these hills rise high in the distance. Upon reaching the highest point of Kitridge lane, at a height of 349m, the road starts descending. From here, for the most part, it is an easy stroll all the way into Withyridge. Keep an eye out on your right for a sign that will lead you through a gate and into a field.

G Once through this gate, head directly straight up and over through the first meadow, and onwards through the next few fields. Just keep heading towards the gates, until you eventually come out into a lane adjacent to the Withypool's old school house. Head down the lane to come out behind the local store, follow the road around to the left and then head down the first set of steps. You are now on the main road that runs through Withypool.

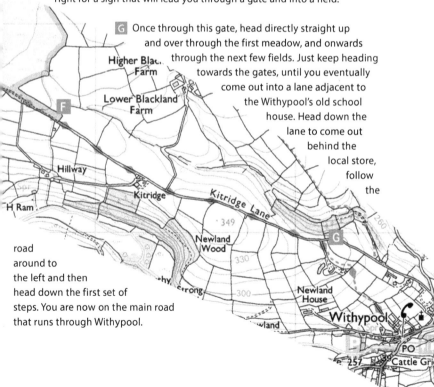

Withypool

OS Grid Ref: SS 8443 3535
District: West Somerset
OS Explorer map: OL9: Exmoor

Distance: 9.6km / 5.9miles
Elevation Gain: 143m

Points of Interests
- Public Car Park
- Withypool Village Shop

Accommodation and eateries
- Withypool Tea Rooms
- The Royal Oak
- Westerclose House Cottages
- Kings Farm
- Fir Tree Farm

Tarr Steps
Points of Interests
- Public Toilets
- Public Car Park (Charges apply)
- Tarr Steps

Accommodation and eateries
- Tarr Farm Inn

Formerly known as Widipol, Withhypoole, or Widepolle, Withypool, like Simonsbath, this village is again located in Somerset and is equally home to a low number of residents – approximately 201 folks as of 2011. Withypool is also located in the Barle Valley and has been inhabited since the Bronze Age. The Withypool Stone Circle is a testament to this. Interestingly, in the fourteenth century, the 'father of English Literature', Geoffrey Chaucer, was in charge of this small village. As far as sites to see go, the Withypool bridge, also known as new bridge, is a nice little addition to your journey as you can play pooh-sticks over the River Barle. There are also several other short walks located around the area to enjoy.

Withypool also hosts a shop with a Post Office that stock a good supply of products. It would be a good idea to stock up here because by this point, you should be running low. Withypool also boasts a tearoom which, at the time of writing, is open every day from 9am - 5:30am from spring through to the end of autumn. An excellent place to stop and refuel! Or, if it takes your fancy, there is the local pub, The Royal Oak. The pub provides a decent dining menu as well as a bed & breakfast if you plan on having Withypool as one of your overnight stops.

A Leaving Withypool you should head east along Room Hill Road, passing both St Andrew's Church and the Royal Oak Inn. As you continue along you will eventually arrive at the start of a hill leading out of Withypool. With a 20% gradient, it is quite steep, thankfully you do not have to worry though as it is only roughly 180m until the stile. As you climb the hill you will pass a trail leading off to Exford on your left. This is clearly signposted. B Keep going up the hill another few metres until you finally come to the stile on the right-hand side with the familiar marked signpost of the Two Moors Way directing you to the Tarr Steps. Once you have successfully climbed over the stile, take a second to take in the wonderful view of WIthypool Hill over the other side of the valley. If you head along the path a few metres you can look back and see an equally lovely view of the village below.

From here the route to Tarr Steps is very easy to follow as it is clearly signposted and follows the river's edge all the way. You will initially head through woodland, pass over a stream then turn right at the gate. From here the path gently descends downwards to meet and run alongside the River Barle. Here, you shall then enter your first large clearing with Ham Wood over to your left. C Keep an eye out on your right for the stepping stones that cross the river and lead up to the base of Withypool Hill. Should you wish to deviate from the path across this route, be

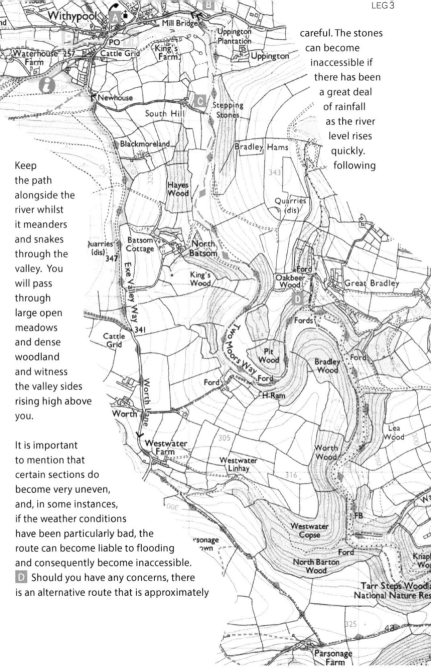

careful. The stones can become inaccessible if there has been a great deal of rainfall as the river level rises quickly. following

Keep the path alongside the river whilst it meanders and snakes through the valley. You will pass through large open meadows and dense woodland and witness the valley sides rising high above you.

It is important to mention that certain sections do become very uneven, and, in some instances, if the weather conditions have been particularly bad, the route can become liable to flooding and consequently become inaccessible. **D** Should you have any concerns, there is an alternative route that is approximately

43

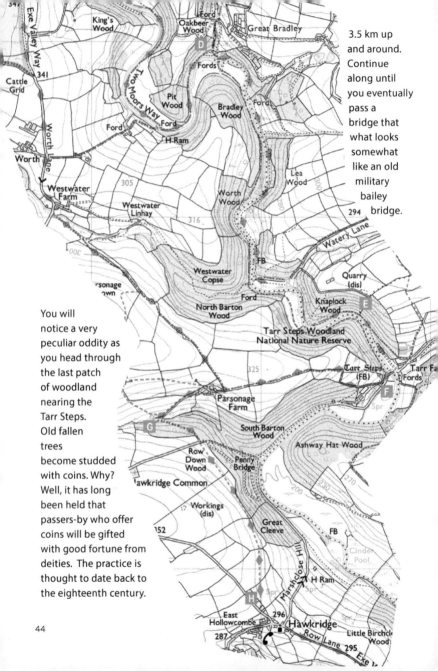

3.5 km up and around. Continue along until you eventually pass a bridge that what looks somewhat like an old military bailey bridge.

You will notice a very peculiar oddity as you head through the last patch of woodland nearing the Tarr Steps. Old fallen trees become studded with coins. Why? Well, it has long been held that passers-by who offer coins will be gifted with good fortune from deities. The practice is thought to date back to the eighteenth century.

E After passing the coined trees you will arrive at a fork in the path. Note, it does not tremendously matter which direction you take here. If you carry on alongside the river you will arrive into a clearing from where you should just be able to make out the Tarr Steps. Otherwise, taking the left fork, you end up entering through into the tea garden of the Tarr Farm Inn. Again, this Inn offers another excellent stop over point and serves a fine selection of food. If you find yourself arriving at a time when The Tarr Farm Inn happens to be closed, then approximately 500m up the road are public toilets and a car park which is operated by the Exmoor National Park Authority. The car park is open 24hrs Monday to Sunday and charges £2 for the day.

Tarr Steps

Clapper bridges, made out of stone or granite slabs, can be found in various parts of the UK. While some date back to the ancient era, most were established in the medieval times. The Tarr Steps clapper bridge is a seventeen segment stone crossing that spans the River Barle. It is the longest of its type in Britain and has been awarded a grade one listed building and scheduled ancient monument status by English Heritage.

The Tarr Steps has, in more recent times, succumbed to the elements. As recently as 2012 and 2016 the bridge was badly damaged by floodwater which washed sections of the bridge away. Thankfully, the local authorities soon restored these sections.

F Once you have walked over the Tarr Steps, take the right fork signposted in the road that heads up the hill and bends around to the right. Once around the bend, you will be greeted with a driveway on your left; the path continues straight up and marks a significant incline. Keep going until you reach a gate at the top and enter through it into the field. Again, keep to the track and head up to the next gate while keeping an eye out for the sign directing you left as this will lead you through another field before finally reaching Parsonage Farm.

A number of bridleways and public footpaths branch off from the farm so it is easy to go astray if you are not careful. Simply stay on the road that heads through Parsonage Farm and leads downhill to a stream. **G** The road here appears as if it nearly turns back on itself. From the stream, head up another short incline where you come to a T-junction. Look for the signpost directing you through the gate.

Once through the gate, head into the field. Though the path will become faint, it should still be visible thanks to the flattened grass along the route. Continue straight towards the gorse bushes where the path turns into a dirt track. You will be elevated at this point and consequently have a beautiful vantage point of the valley beyond. You should be able to spot the car park that sits just up from the Tarr Steps in the distance as well as a glimpse of the River Barle flowing directly below you.

As you head onwards, the gaps in the hedgerows offer more alluring views of the valley below. Cross over a stile and into another field towards the gap in the hedgerow that is straight ahead. Once through and into the next field you should be able to spot a house in the distance. Head towards it while keeping an eye out for the familiar posts with yellow or blue squares. [H] When you finally reach the house you will be greeted by another stile that crosses into what looks like someone's garden and through a little walkway. After entering the gate, you are met with a little wooden bench; an excellent time to take five for a water and food break. Welcome to Hawkridge!

Tarr Steps

Stile leading to Hawkridge

LEG 4 – HAWKRIDGE TO KNOWSTONE

Hawkridge

OS Grid Ref: SS 86050 30683
District: West Somerset
OS Explorer map: OL9: Exmoor

Distance: 10km / 6.2miles
Elevation Gain: 279m

Points of Interests
- St Giles Church
- Hawkridge Village Hall

Accommodation and eateries
- West Hollowcombe
- Zeal Farm
(Located just outside Hawkridge)

Hawkridge, located in the same civil parish as Withypool, is a charming little village that lies high among the hills of Southern Exmoor. It is one of the most beautiful places to spot both the Exmoor pony and red deer. It is also a perfect location to watch the night sky as it is part of Exmoor's International Dark Sky Reserve initiative: no streetlights exist and there is limited light pollution. While in the village, it is worth visiting the Norman Church of St Giles as its fourteenth-century origins make for a wonderful example of historic architecture. The village, and its surrounding areas, also offer great cycling routes, fishing areas, shooting ranges, and horse riding opportunities.

Exmoor Dark Sky Reserve

Due to the rural nature of Exmoor, it is one of the few places in England to have such low light pollution levels. Given this, you are able to gaze up in awe and wonder at the majesty of the night sky. Exmoor has even been awarded the International Dark Sky Reserve accolade. Exmoor is the first place in Europe to be awarded such status.

A After encountering the large tree and water pump in the centre of Hawkridge, you will notice the hills of West Anstey Common rising high directly in front of you; these are your next goal. Turn right along Broad Lane past the village hall and continue along until you turn a corner and see the sign for West Hollowcombe; you will notice a stone bench outside the drive. Directly to the right is a gate which is where the path leads. Upon entering the field there is very little evidence on which way the path actually heads off, but you should head right ensuring not to venture too far down into the field. Keep an eye out for a gate approximately half way down the hedgerow as this leads out into Slade Lane.

B Upon joining Slade Lane turn left and proceed downhill into the valley. The Danes Brook river flows through here and eventually merges into the River Barle. At the bottom of the valley is where you'll be waving goodbye and leaving Somerset behind as you cross over Slade Bridge into Devon.

Here you will begin a steep ascent up Venford Hill. Once level with a gate on your left, look directly opposite on the right-hand side where you should see a post with the MW marker. **C** Crossover and continue up-hill joining onto West Anstey Common. The track ascends around to the left where you will finally join a solid gravel track. **D** After a further approximate 600m, crossover Ridge Road; it runs along the top of East and West Anstey Common. Once over descend through Woodland Common to be eventually greeted by **E** one-half of the unusual and beautiful sculptures that marks the entry point to Exmoor National Park.

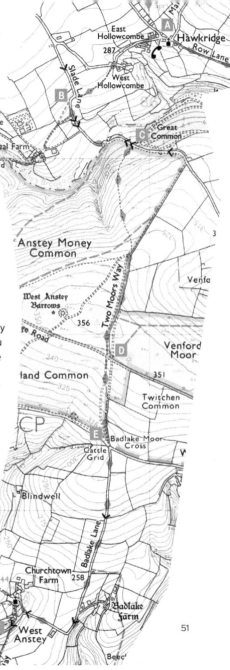

IIMW sculpture

The IIMW sculpture was created by Peter Randall-Page. The sculpture was commissioned by Devon County council in 2004. It is situated facing its sister half which can be found at the bottom of an ancient track near to Drewsteignton; you will pass this later on the route.

Follow Badlake Lane down into West Anstey bypassing the St Petrock Church. **F** As you head past the old vicarage, look out for the gate to the left leading into a field. Enter through the gate and proceed up and over through a number of fields and along a bridleway. You'll eventually arrive on to Dunsley Hill. **G** From here, turn right and again stick to the road until you eventually see the large farm buildings and the giveaway sign on your left for Yeo Mill. Venturing into Yeo Mill, keep to the main road and keep heading straight through the old railway bridge for approximately 700m. Yeo Mill is another very small rural community with not much in the way of facilities, only a village hall.

51

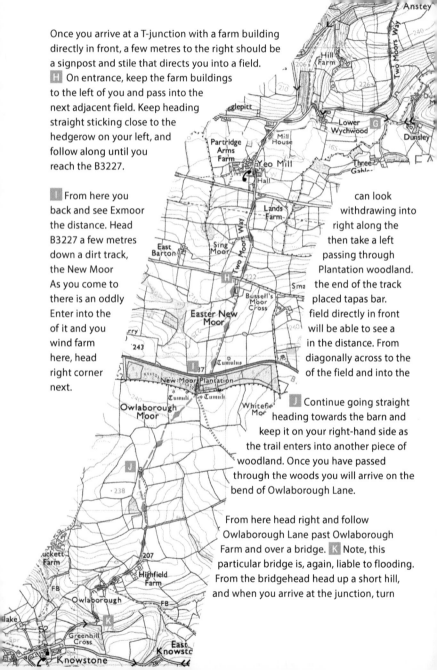

Once you arrive at a T-junction with a farm building directly in front, a few metres to the right should be a signpost and stile that directs you into a field. **H** On entrance, keep the farm buildings to the left of you and pass into the next adjacent field. Keep heading straight sticking close to the hedgerow on your left, and follow along until you reach the B3227.

I From here you ⋯ back and see Exmoor ⋯ the distance. Head ⋯ B3227 a few metres ⋯ down a dirt track, ⋯ the New Moor ⋯ As you come to ⋯ there is an oddly ⋯ Enter into the ⋯ of it and you ⋯ wind farm ⋯ here, head ⋯ right corner ⋯ next.

⋯ can look ⋯ withdrawing into ⋯ right along the ⋯ then take a left ⋯ passing through ⋯ Plantation woodland. ⋯ the end of the track ⋯ placed tapas bar. ⋯ field directly in front ⋯ will be able to see a ⋯ in the distance. From ⋯ diagonally across to the ⋯ of the field and into the

J Continue going straight heading towards the barn and keep it on your right-hand side as the trail enters into another piece of woodland. Once you have passed through the woods you will arrive on the bend of Owlaborough Lane.

From here head right and follow Owlaborough Lane past Owlaborough Farm and over a bridge. **K** Note, this particular bridge is, again, liable to flooding. From the bridgehead head up a short hill, and when you arrive at the junction, turn right and proceed into Knowstone. You will be greeted with The Masons Arms on your right, and St Peters Church directly opposite on your left.

IIMW Sculpture

Knowstone

OS Grid Ref: SS 8265 2306
District: North Devon
OS Explorer map: 114: Exeter & the Exe
Valley

Distance: 12km / 7.5miles
Elevation Gain: 172m

Points of Interest
- Church of St Peter
- Knowstone Village Hall

Accommodation and eateries
- The Masons Arms
- Little Owl Cottage B&B
- Rosemary Cottage B&B

Buses
Exe Valley Market and Community Bus EV2,
Oakford – South Molton
(Alternate Thursdays only)

Exe Valley Market and Community Bus EV3,
Oakford – Barnstaple
(Alternate Thursdays only)

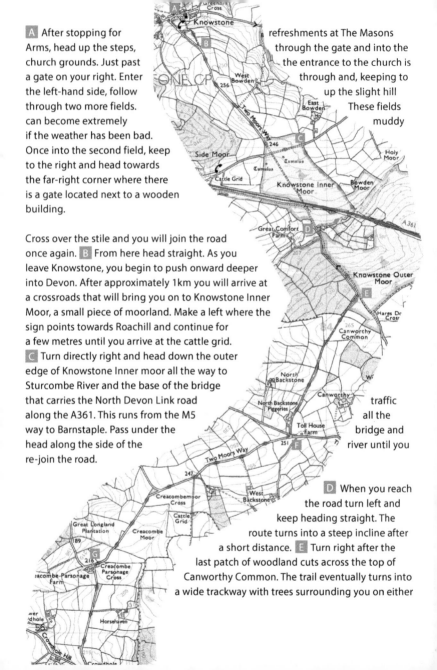

A After stopping for refreshments at The Masons Arms, head up the steps, through the gate and into the church grounds. Just past the entrance to the church is a gate on your right. Enter through and, keeping to the left-hand side, follow up the slight hill through two more fields. These fields can become extremely muddy if the weather has been bad. Once into the second field, keep to the right and head towards the far-right corner where there is a gate located next to a wooden building.

Cross over the stile and you will join the road once again. **B** From here head straight. As you leave Knowstone, you begin to push onward deeper into Devon. After approximately 1km you will arrive at a crossroads that will bring you on to Knowstone Inner Moor, a small piece of moorland. Make a left where the sign points towards Roachill and continue for a few metres until you arrive at the cattle grid. **C** Turn directly right and head down the outer edge of Knowstone Inner moor all the way to Sturcombe River and the base of the bridge that carries the North Devon Link road along the A361. This runs from the M5 traffic way to Barnstaple. Pass under the all the head along the side of the bridge re-join the road. river until you

D When you reach the road turn left and keep heading straight. The route turns into a steep incline after a short distance. **E** Turn right after the last patch of woodland cuts across the top of Canworthy Common. The trail eventually turns into a wide trackway with trees surrounding you on either

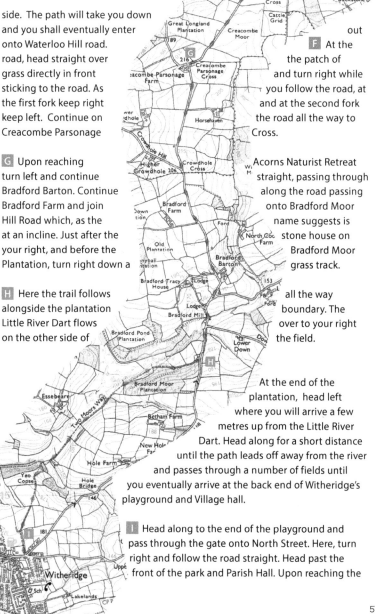

side. The path will take you down
and you shall eventually enter
onto Waterloo Hill road.
road, head straight over
grass directly in front
sticking to the road. As
the first fork keep right
keep left. Continue on
Creacombe Parsonage

out
F At the
the patch of
and turn right while
you follow the road, at
and at the second fork
the road all the way to
Cross.

G Upon reaching
turn left and continue
Bradford Barton. Continue
Bradford Farm and join
Hill Road which, as the
at an incline. Just after the
your right, and before the
Plantation, turn right down a

Acorns Naturist Retreat
straight, passing through
along the road passing
onto Bradford Moor
name suggests is
stone house on
Bradford Moor
grass track.

H Here the trail follows
alongside the plantation
Little River Dart flows
on the other side of

all the way to
boundary. The
over to your right
the field.

At the end of the
plantation, head left
where you will arrive a few
metres up from the Little River
Dart. Head along for a short distance
until the path leads off away from the river
and passes through a number of fields until
you eventually arrive at the back end of Witheridge's
playground and Village hall.

I Head along to the end of the playground and
pass through the gate onto North Street. Here, turn
right and follow the road straight. Head past the
front of the park and Parish Hall. Upon reaching the

crossroads take the first right; this is the B3137 and is the main route through Witheridge. Head down until you reach the village square. Here you will find the village amenities along with the main bus route, the 155 bus, that serves onwards travel to either Barnstaple or Exeter via Tiverton.

St Peter's Church, Knowstone

A361 flyover

LEG 6 – WITHERIDGE TO MORCHARD BISHOP

Witheridge

Witheridge OS Grid Ref: SS 8047 1447
District: North Devon
OS Explorer map: 113: Okehampton

Distance: 11.5km / 7.1miles
Elevation Gain: 196m

Points of Interests
- Witheridge Post Office & Stores
- Witheridge Newsagents
- Mole Valley Farmers
- Village Hall
- Public Toilets

Accommodation and eateries
- The Mire Inn
- Angel of Witheridge Pub – Café
- Rockhaye Cottage B&B
(Located just outside Witheridge)

Buses
Stagecoach 155,
Exeter – Barnstaple (Monday to Saturday)

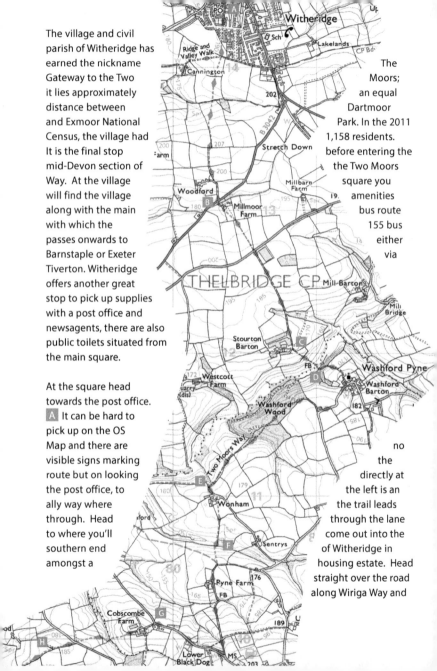

The village and civil parish of Witheridge has earned the nickname Gateway to the Two it lies approximately distance between and Exmoor National Census, the village had It is the final stop mid-Devon section of Way. At the village will find the village along with the main with which the passes onwards to Barnstaple or Exeter Tiverton. Witheridge offers another great stop to pick up supplies with a post office and newsagents, there are also public toilets situated from the main square.

At the square head towards the post office. It can be hard to pick up on the OS Map and there are visible signs marking route but on looking the post office, to ally way where through. Head to where you'll southern end amongst a

The Moors; an equal Dartmoor Park. In the 2011 1,158 residents. before entering the the Two Moors square you amenities bus route 155 bus either via

no the directly at the left is an the trail leads through the lane come out into the of Witheridge in housing estate. Head straight over the road along Wiriga Way and at the end of the road you'll spot a gate directly below a telegraph pole at the start of a drive. Enter into the field and head straight passing over a small stream and through an additional number of other meadows, the part is well sign posted. You'll eventually arrive at the drive way to Woodford farm. Head left down the drive a short distance until you reach the B3042. **B** From the junction look right and you'll notice one of the familiar signs pointing left up another drive way that leads to Millmoor Farm. A short distance up the drive pass through the gate into pasture land making your way to the top left of the field. You'll come to another road and directly in front of you will be the large agricultural buildings and grain silos.

Head straight along the track to the right of the silos, crossing over the cattle grid and continue along the lane which takes you into Stourton Barton Farm. **C** Upon reaching the farm keep heading straight and at the end of the large building make a left just before another cattle grid, then directly right where the path will curve around to the left. As you enter into small field look directly right, down the hill, where you should be able to see a wooden gate, where the trail leads. **D** When you pass through the gate you should be able to spot a wooden bridge directly ahead. There are numerous tracks leading off left and right. But just head straight down the hill and over the stream. On the other side of the stream head upwards through a small patch of woodland to arrive out into the back end of Washford Pyne, which is a tiny village, a collection of houses and agricultural buildings. You'll be able to spot the steeple of the church of St Peter, a church which dates back to the 15th century.

E Cross over the road and enter through another gate directly in front. At the end of the farm building go towards the bottom right of the field and proceed into the next field along and keep close to the hedge row that leads down to a wooden bridge, cross the bridge and head up a short steep incline and through the gate. Once you're in the next field there are no obvious tracks or signs informing you which way to go. **F** However head directly straight up and upon reaching the brow of the hill you'll spot a three-way public bridleway sign. Once at the sign look forwards and head towards the gate head along another narrow dirt track until you reach the buildings of Pyne Farm. From here just head along the drive way that leads all the way down Copstone Hill and into Lower Black Dog. Upon reaching the junction turn right where there are a collection of houses.

G Head along Copstone hill leaving Lower Black Dog and after a few hundred metres on your left, you'll spot a sign post and gate where the path leads through

Leading to Brook Rd

Heading through Pyne Farm

into a field. Once through the gate head along the hedge line leading straight until you come to a gate on your left. From the field turn right and venture down the hill a few metres and turn left, then head forwards bypassing a large pit with blocks of slate on your left. Head downwards towards a gate and a wooden bridge and cross over into the next field. The trail then heads upwards to join on to a road where you need to cross over in to the adjacent field. **H** Follow the dirt track up to the barn keeping to the hedge line on your left and continue along until you reach another small patch of woodland.

I As you reach the woodland there are wooden planks leading to a wooden bridge, to help you traverse through into the next field as the ground around this area is extremely water logged and muddy. Once across the bridge head to the bottom left of the field, into the next and turn left again.

Head straight until you arrive at the road, once at the road and directly ahead you'll see the sign pointing to Lower Brownstone Farm. **J** Head down the drive way, keeping an eye out on your right for a gate that leads into an meadow which leads right hand side You'll come with that

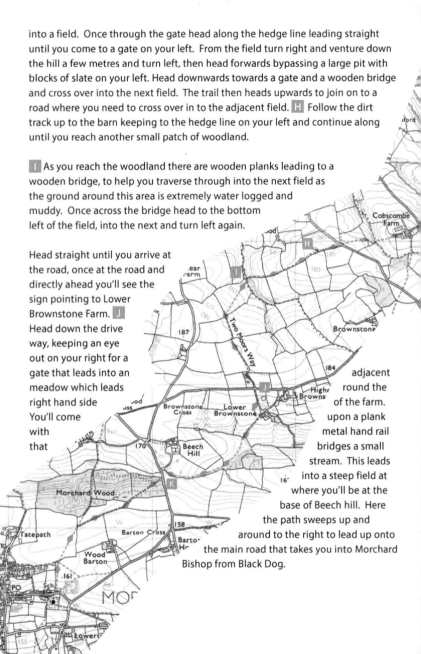

adjacent round the of the farm. upon a plank metal hand rail bridges a small stream. This leads into a steep field at where you'll be at the base of Beech hill. Here the path sweeps up and around to the right to lead up onto the main road that takes you into Morchard Bishop from Black Dog.

K Upon reaching the road you'll now be at the bottom of Cuckoo Hill, next to large black metal gates. Look towards the woodland on your left and head along the road for just a few metres and take the immediate right and enter into Morchard Wood. The trail leads upwards to bring you out on top of the hill where you'll be able to see St Mary's Church and the roof tops of houses peering through the trees. It's then a leisurely stroll all the way into the public car park that's situated directly next to the primary school and St Mary's Church.

Beech Hill

LEG 7 – MORCHARD BISHOP TO DREWSTEIGNTON

Morchard Bishop

OS Grid Ref: SS 7697 0752
District: Mid-Devon
OS Explorer map: 113: Okehampton

Distance: 24.5km / 15.2 miles
Elevation Gain: 569 m

Points of Interest
- Mary's Church
- Public Car Park
- Memorial Hall
- Church Street Stores

Accommodation and eateries
- The London Inn

Train Station
Located at Morchard Road

Buses
Turners Tours 369,
Chumleigh - Exeter (Monday to Saturday)

Located in Mid Devon, with a population of 975 residents, Morchard Bishop is yet another small village and civil parish that you will stroll through while walking the Two Moors Way. Further, with over forty different footpaths, Morchard Bishop has one of the highest numbers of public footpaths of any parish in Devon, thus making it a perfect place to explore the wider countryside. The area is also home to the Church of St Mary, a sixteenth-century religious institution with a 95-foot tower. If you are looking to join the Two Moors Way en route, there is a nearby train station at Morchard Road, situated roughly 4km along the A377, the road running from Exeter to Barnstaple.

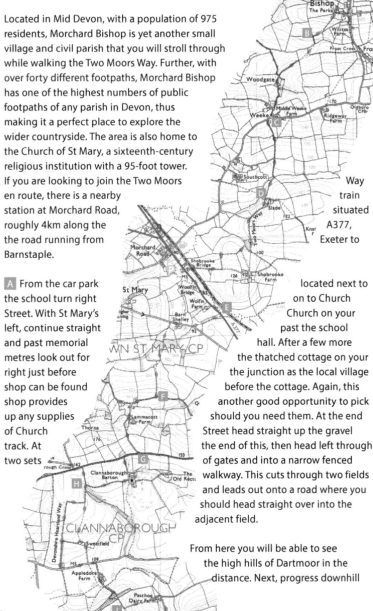

A From the car park located next to the school turn right on to Church Street. With St Mary's Church on your left, continue straight past the school and past memorial hall. After a few more metres look out for the thatched cottage on your right just before the junction as the local village shop can be found before the cottage. Again, this shop provides another good opportunity to pick up any supplies should you need them. At the end of Church Street head straight up the gravel track. At the end of this, then head left through two sets of gates and into a narrow fenced walkway. This cuts through two fields and leads out onto a road where you should head straight over into the adjacent field.

From here you will be able to see the high hills of Dartmoor in the distance. Next, progress downhill

Leading towards Woodgate

keeping to
path around
you reach the
to the proceeding
dirt path will then
takes you through
Weeke. **C** Once
Down Hill, turn
runs in front of the
reach a wooden
D Accompanied
a small area of
eventually happen
patch of land with
Slade Farm. Head
leading away from
and turn left at the
proceed past the
to come back to
Next, follow the
next field and
far right corner to
track. Cross over
and follow the
way down
Bridge.
passes

the left-hand side and follow the
as it bends to the right. **B** When
gate, turn right and head down
gate then turn right again. The
lead you into the narrow lane that
a hamlet, Woodgate, and on into
at the junction that joins onto
right then take the left lane that
house and follow it until you
plank bridging a stream.
by a gate leading through to
trees, advance forward until you
upon a very peaceful, large open
two small lakes that belong to
up onto the track and proceed right
the farm. Cross over the cattle grid
end of the fence. Head straight and
small wooded area and turn right
the other side of the woodland.
hedge line around into the
head up towards the
meet up with a
the cattle grid
track all the
to Shobrooke
This bridge
over the main
railway line
from Exeter to
Barnstaple. On the
other side of the bridge
proceed through the gate on
the left.

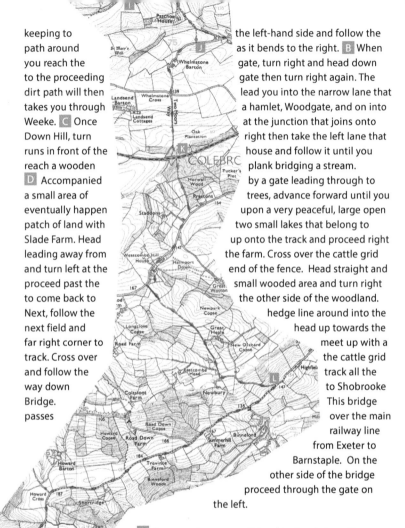

E Once you have passed the gate, head along the
narrow grassy walkway that runs alongside the A377. Keep
an eye out on your right-hand side as you will eventually
arrive at a gate that opens out on to the A377 itself. Take extra
precaution here as it is often an extremely fast road. Cross straight

over the A377 and turn left along the verge for a few metres before proceeding right through another gate into the field. Head straight following the hedge line until you arrive out into Barn Hill. Turn right and walk along the road until you pass Barn Shelly Lodge. After a few metres take a left and enter into a field.

Proceed through a small patch of woodland until you encounter a wide dirt track that runs around the edge of the field. Head right and follow the track up onto Lammacott Lane. **F** Turn right until you pass a barn on your right and take the next left after it. Continue onwards passing Lammacott Farm until you eventually enter out on to the A3072. Again, please remember to take extra care as it is a fast-moving main A road that runs from Copplestone, through to Bow, and onward to the north of Okehampton.

G At this stage, you will now be deep in the area known as Mid Devon. At the A3072 turn right, walk along the grass verge then take the first left; it is only a short distance. Next, head down towards the farm shop until you reach the medieval church of St Petrock. Proceed over the cattle grid and into the field directly opposite the church and head along the wide dirt track. Pass the barn and make a small loop around to the left. **H** This is where the long-distance walk, the Devonshire Heartland Way, joins up with the Two Moors Way for a short distance. Here you should head directly south and the path will cut straight across the middle of a field, directly towards the cottages in the distance. Proceed until you reach the hedge line in front of these cottages.

At the cottages turn left and proceed around the side of the buildings. Once through into the next field head straight until the road is on the other side of the hedge. Head left a short distance and enter out onto the road. At the road turn right and head back on yourself until the left turn through into Appledore Farm; the trail takes you straight through the farm itself. At the end of the last building take the middle dirt track as this leads up and around to the right passing through a small wooded area.

I Once you have made it through the woodland, take the next left and head down into Paschoe Dairy Farm. Cross over the road that leads into the grounds of Paschoe House, and turn right. From here the path leads up and around the left-hand side of the grounds. After passing the house there is a slight incline – here, the Devonshire Heartland Way forks left and continues onwards to the final destination of Stoke Cannon, keep right though and head up onto another narrow country lane.

J At Ford Hill turn right and follow the road until you reach the junction. Cross straight over and head down a narrow dirt path that leads to a stream with a small bridge, then proceed to the level crossing at the railway line.

The Exeter to Plymouth railway of the London and South Western Railway

This stretch of railway runs from Okehampton to Exeter. It was originally built during the 1860s and served commuters where it passed through the towns of Crediton, Okehampton and Tavistock and on to Plymouth. It was eventually axed in 1973 leaving just local services at either end.

K Head into Horwell Wood until eventually entering out onto a country lane next to Parkeham Farm. Turn right and walk until you pass Westcombe House. A short distance after, and just before Common Plantation, follow the track leading to the left and continue through various fields. Eventually, you will arrive at a gate that leads back onto a solid road and serves as access to the surrounding houses. Proceed along the road. After a little way, this road turns into a considerable incline and leads up to a junction. Here you will find a welcome rest point at the top in the form of a raised grassy island in the middle of the intersection.

L At the top take a sharp right then it is simply a case of following the road along for about 4km all the way into Hittisleigh. M When you arrive at the crossroads continue straight on, past the public telephone box and until the two thatched cottages on your left. Take the left track between the cottages and alongside Newhouse Lane until you reach Whiteford Farm. Just as you have passed the last of the farm buildings, turn right and head through more meadows working your way through to Hill Farm. At Hill Farm head around the left side and follow downhill until you reach a country lane. Turn right then take the next left onto the gravel track.

The path leads through woodland and onwards across various meadows, all of which are well signposted. Eventually, you will pass a barn on your right whilst climbing up to join alongside the A30. At the top of the hill follow the track around to the right to where it joins up on to Hask Lane. Turn left, head over the bridge that crosses over the A30, and, after a short distance take the first right and head all the way down to Winscombe Farm, ensuring you keep right. After passing the final barn head down the grassy track with hedgerows either side. Here you find the other half of the IIMW Sculpture facing towards East Antsy Common. Proceed through the woodland to come out at the side of Veet Mill Farm.

Enter through the gate adjacent to the driveway and head right over the tiny bridge directly in front. From here the road starts to steepen considerably after a short distance. A very lengthy incline takes you all the way into Drewsteignton, just follow the road. Eventually, you will be right in the centre of the village where you can now take a much deserved rest.

Cottages

LEG 8 – DREWSTEIGNTON TO WIDECOMBE-IN-THE-MOOR

Drewsteignton

OS Grid Ref: SX 7371 9083
District: West Devon
OS Explorer map: OL28: Dartmoor

Distance: 25km / 15.5miles
Elevation Gain: 634m

Points of Interest
- Public Car Park
- Holy Trinity Church
- Post Office and Stores

Accommodation and eateries
- The Old Inn
- The Drewe Arms
- Rookwood Cottage

Buses
Dartline 173 (Monday - Saturday)
Moretonhampstead - Exeter

Castle Drogo
Café and Public Toilets

The civil parish, village, and former manor area of Drewsteignton dates back to the Neolithic period and is a populated by 1,616 people. Located in the valley of the River Teign, Drewsteignton lies within Dartmoor National Park. There are several things to see and do in the nearby area: visitors can enjoy an Iron Age hill fort, Neolithic burial chambers, Fingle Bridge, and Spinster's Rock. Most popular, however, is the National Trust's Castle Drogo. Overlooking the Teign Gorge, the castle is currently undergoing a conservation project to make it watertight. Constructed between 1911 and 1930, it was the last castle to be built in England. Julius Drewe, founder Castle Drogo, is buried in the village churchyard in Drewsteignton.

A From the square lead off down the road facing directly away from the post office. Keep the telephone box on your left, and follow the road around to the right. After passing the last house follow the stone wall along for a few metres then turn left onto a stony track. Head along the lane and follow the bend to the right and continue down into a patch of woodland. Here, cross over the stream and follow up the steep hill. Note, there is a diversion that leads around to the left, however, the climb is fairly short. Once through the trees head directly straight across the wide-open fields. If you wanted to plan in a stop off at Castle Drogo, then after the first field there is a track leading off to the Castle. The National Trust looks after it and offers facilities such as a café and toilets.

B Upon reaching the ridgeline of Teign gorge, head right passing over Sharp Tor. From here you will have a spectacular view overlooking the steep wooded gorge that the River Teign flows through. On the other side of the valley, and to your left, will be Hannicombe Wood. On your right is Whiddon Wood. There are several footpaths that cut through these surrounding woodlands that lead down to and around Fingle Bridge, an old 17th century packhorse bridge.

As you continue along the ridgeline you will pass just below Castle Drogo and eventually loop back round to the right, over Hunters Tor, and end up facing the west side of the castle. From here, the path leads down to a public access driveway. Upon joining the road, take a left and head down the drive, keeping left bypassing Coombe Farm on your right, until you end up at the River Teign.

C Upon reaching the water's edge, turn right and follow the path that runs alongside the river through more large pasture lands. When you reach Dogmarsh Bridge, cross straight over the A382 and into the next field. The path continues to follow the river through more woodland and fields until you eventually arrive at Rushford Mill Farm. D Once out onto the road turn left and head past Chagford's Swimming pool. Continue straight until you stop short of the next bridge, turn right through the gate into the field. From here the path is well trodden; the grass will be worn but is still easy to follow. After a short distance, you will return to the River Teign as it flows around the north of Chagford.

E Upon reaching the road once again, turn left and proceed over the bridge. Pass along the extremely narrow lane until you arrive at a junction. Take the very first right, you will see a sign stating that it is 'unsuitable for heavy goods vehicles'. Head along the road, and once at the beautifully situated Holystreet Manor, follow the road around to the left to where it starts to turn into a steep incline before levelling to a more gradual ascent. Once at the top, enjoy the beautiful scenery as your wind through

79

the woodland areas. **F** Upon reaching a bend in the road, with the large sign for 'Gidleigh Park Hotel & Restaurant', a wide dirt track leads uphill off to the left. Littered with trees each side, head up the dirt track.

When you emerge onto the driveway, follow it down to the point that it joins with the main country lane and head directly straight. **G** Keep to the road and you will arrive in Teigncombe. Once in Teigncombe, keeping left, continue straight. The main road will bend around to the right. After passing the last house, enter through the gate on your left into a field. From here the route takes you on a delightful walk through dense woodland, over streams, and across numerous meadows all the way down through into Great Frenchbeer. In the spring months, you will see hundreds of bluebells littered along this part of the route. High above up to your right will be Chagford Common, including Kestor Rock and Middle Tor. **H** Once at the road head straight across in-between the farm buildings of Frenchbeer Farm. Continue along the hedge line, turn left, then after a few metres, take a right. Keeping close to the tree line, proceed and cross the footbridge at the South Teign River. Once over the bridge pass through the remaining fields to enter out into Yardworthy Farm. At the farm proceed left until the end of the driveway.

I At this point, the Two Moors Way splits in two. You should be able to see stone steps leading up to a stile directly ahead: this route leads all the way down into Widecombe-in-the-moor passing through much of the similar gentle terrain that you just previously encountered; mostly

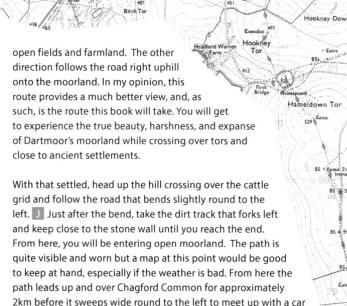

open fields and farmland. The other direction follows the road right uphill onto the moorland. In my opinion, this route provides a much better view, and, as such, is the route this book will take. You will get to experience the true beauty, harshness, and expanse of Dartmoor's moorland while crossing over tors and close to ancient settlements.

With that settled, head up the hill crossing over the cattle grid and follow the road that bends slightly round to the left. **J** Just after the bend, take the dirt track that forks left and keep close to the stone wall until you reach the end. From here, you will be entering open moorland. The path is quite visible and worn but a map at this point would be good to keep at hand, especially if the weather is bad. From here the path leads up and over Chagford Common for approximately 2km before it sweeps wide round to the left to meet up with a car park located on the other side of the B3212. This road runs from the suburbs of Exeter across Dartmoor and on down to Plymouth. To your right on this stretch, you will see Fenworthy Forest and its reservoir.

K When you arrive at the carpark, the trail leads off to the left, up and over the back end of Birch Tor, then down again to join up with a road. At the road, cross straight over and follow the path around and up through the centre of Hookeney Tor, offering a great view of the prehistoric settlement of Grimspound below.

Head down towards the settlement. Passing it to the right, then ascend up
Hameldown Tor (532m). Once at the top, follow the ridgeline of Hameldown in
a southerly direction for approximately 3km, passing Hameldown Beacon in the
process. L Once the path joins up with a stone wall on your left, you should
follow the track around to its left and descend until you reach a road. This road
takes you down into Widecombe in the Moor. Though you could bypass the village
and continue straight on, Widecombe is definitely worth visiting, even if you do
not need to pick up provisions.

Near Castle Drogo

Leading towards Great Frenchbeer

LEG 9 – WIDECOMBE-IN-THE-MOOR TO HOLNE

Widecombe-in-the-moor

OS Grid Ref: SX 7181 7677
District: Teignbridge
OS Explorer map: OL28: Dartmoor

Distance: 11km / 7miles
Elevation Gain: 346m

Points of Interest
- St Pancras Church
- Village Green
- Public toilets
- Public Car Parks
- Widecombe gifts
- The shop on the green
- National Trust Shop
- D Middleweek – Gift shop

Accommodation and eateries
- The Café on the green
- Wayside Café
- The Old Inn
- The Rugglestone Inn
- Manor Cottage

Buses
Country Bus 271,
Newton Abbot – Widecombe
(Summer Only)

Newton Abbot Community Transport 627
Newton Abbot - Buckland in the Moor
(Wednesdays Only)

Located deep within Dartmoor, the charming village of Widecombe-in-the-moor, is, as the name suggests, surrounded by high moorland. Widecombe is home to the gorgeous Church of St Pancras. Made from nearby quarried granite in the fourteenth century, the Church has colloquially been dubbed the "Cathedral of the Moors" thanks to its 120-foot tower. Badly damaged in the Great Thunderstorm of 1638, legend holds the Devil visited this area. The village is also home to several events through the year, most famously the Widecombe Fair. Held annually on the second Tuesday in September, this fair displays various livestock, local produce, rural arts and crafts, and a dog show.

Widecombe-in-the-moor Annual Fair

The Widecombe fair has continued to grow in popularity over the years. The earliest records are from 1850. Originally, the fair started as a place where local farmers brought their cattle to sell. It quickly progressed into an opportunity to show off locally bred animals. By the 1920s, the fair incorporated the local school sports day into the event. Today, you will still continue to see high-quality livestock as well as vintage machinery, arts and crafts, and many stalls selling local produce. More details can be found by visiting the official website: (www.widecombefair.com)

A Starting at Widecombe green, follow the road south along the B3387, beyond the Old Inn and the Smithy Fine Ceramics shop, pass the post box on your right, and follow the road as it arcs to the left. Head past the Widecombe Primary School and take the next right where the signage will point you to Southcombe. Here, you will be confronted with an extremely steep climb that will enable you to get back up onto the moor; it can be quite challenging if you are carrying a heavy pack. **B** Once you reach the stone buildings on your left, you are about halfway. This offers a good rest stop before continuing onwards. When you see a gate on your right is, the hill starts to level off and enters back onto the moorland. Here is a good opportunity to glance behind you as you will be able to see Widecombe, as well as the soaring hills of Pil Tor, Top Tor and Chinkwell Tor.

Keeping to the road or grass verge, continue along the plateau. Over to your left, you will see the top of Wind Tor. The road eventually starts to descend. **C** Upon reaching the crossroads, continue straight over and in-between the stone walls either side. The road becomes quite narrow but you should continue until you

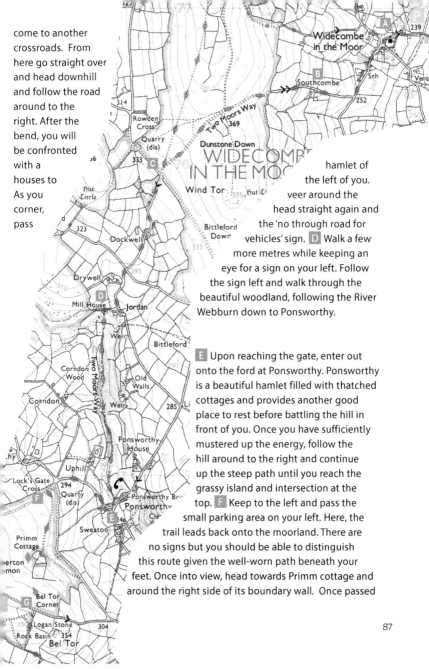

come to another crossroads. From here go straight over and head downhill and follow the road around to the right. After the bend, you will be confronted with a houses to As you corner, pass

hamlet of the left of you. veer around the head straight again and the 'no through road for vehicles' sign. **D** Walk a few more metres while keeping an eye for a sign on your left. Follow the sign left and walk through the beautiful woodland, following the River Webburn down to Ponsworthy.

E Upon reaching the gate, enter out onto the ford at Ponsworthy. Ponsworthy is a beautiful hamlet filled with thatched cottages and provides another good place to rest before battling the hill in front of you. Once you have sufficiently mustered up the energy, follow the hill around to the right and continue up the steep path until you reach the grassy island and intersection at the top. **F** Keep to the left and pass the small parking area on your left. Here, the trail leads back onto the moorland. There are no signs but you should be able to distinguish this route given the well-worn path beneath your feet. Once into view, head towards Primm cottage and around the right side of its boundary wall. Once passed

Aish Tor

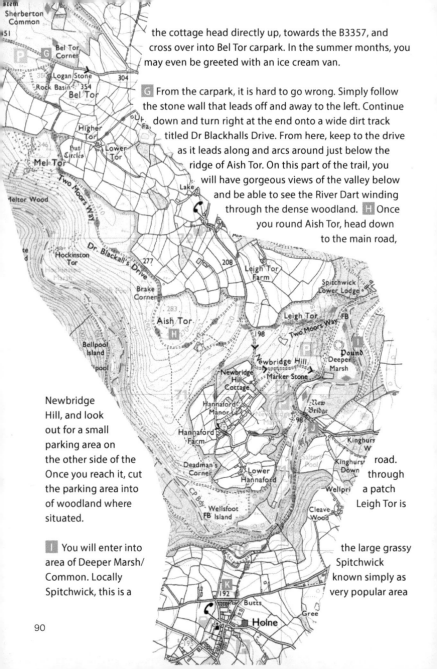

the cottage head directly up, towards the B3357, and cross over into Bel Tor carpark. In the summer months, you may even be greeted with an ice cream van.

G From the carpark, it is hard to go wrong. Simply follow the stone wall that leads off and away to the left. Continue down and turn right at the end onto a wide dirt track titled Dr Blackhalls Drive. From here, keep to the drive as it leads along and arcs around just below the ridge of Aish Tor. On this part of the trail, you will have gorgeous views of the valley below and be able to see the River Dart winding through the dense woodland. **H** Once you round Aish Tor, head down to the main road,

Newbridge Hill, and look out for a small parking area on the other side of the Once you reach it, cut the parking area into of woodland where situated.

I You will enter into area of Deeper Marsh/ Common. Locally Spitchwick, this is a

road. through a patch Leigh Tor is

the large grassy Spitchwick known simply as very popular area and can get extremely crowded during hot summer days as families enjoy picnics and wild swimming. From here, follow the River Dart up to New Bridge carpark. Just before you reach the carpark, take a left and head over the bridge. **J** Turn right into the car parking layby and walk over the wooden footbridge to enter a wooded area. This is another delightful woodland walk as it follows the River Dart upstream slightly before the path branches off. Be sure to stick to the left trail as it leads up through a small number of meadows and enters out into the north side of Holne. **K** At the road, turn left, take the first right, and follow the road a short distance down into the centre of Holne itself.

Leigh Tor

LEG 10 – HOLNE TO IVYBRIDGE

Holne

OS Grid Ref: SX 7045 6938
District: South Hams
OS Explorer map: OL28: Dartmoor

Distance: 21.5km / 13miles
Elevation Gain: 449m

Points of Interest
- St. Mary the Virgin Church
- Holne Village Hall

Accommodation and eateries
- The Church House Inn
- Holne Community Shop & Tea Room
- Walkers Retreat
- The Tradesman's Arms
(Located in Scorriton)
- Mitchelcroft B&B
(Located in Scorriton)
- Wisteria Cottage Dartmoor
(Located in Scorriton)

Buses
Newton Abbot Community Transport,
Newton Abbot - Buckland in the Moor 627
(Wednesdays only)

Holne is a tiny village situated directly south of Widecombe-in-the-moor. With evidence of community life since the eleventh century, Holne is today home to a mere 250 residents. While the River Dart forms the eastern and northern boundaries of the parish, the Dartmoor forest borders the west of the village; the scenery is consequently something of true beauty. In Holne, it is worth visiting the Church of St Mary the Virgin, built around 1300 and enlarged in 1500. I also recommend venturing to see Holne Chase Castle, an Iron Age hill fort located between the medieval bridges of Holne and New Bridge.

A When you reach The Church House Inn, continue along the road past the entrance. A few meters from the pub you will see a sign for the village hall, and the village hall car park will be on your left. Behind the car park, you may also notice a wooden hut; this is the Holne community shop and tea room, run and staffed by volunteers. From the tea shop, the road bends around to the right, follow this road up the hill until you reach a house with a signpost in front. The signpost shows Hexworthy is to your right, and Scorriton is down the hill to the left. Take the left towards Scorriton, and, after approximately 100m, follow the main road as it bends around to the right and you should see a dirt track straight ahead.

Follow the dirt road downhill to Langaford where you join a solid road again. Head around to the right and cross over the small bridge that the Holy Brook Stream flows beneath. Immediately after the bridge, take the next right and head up the narrow lane into Scorriton. Sticking to the road head straight until you come to a T-junction. B There will be a telephone box on your left, and three public benches straight ahead as well as a post box, and a rubbish bin.

From the junction turn right, then take a sharp left. If you wish to visit The Tradesman's Arms pub for a drink or a bite to eat, instead of taking the left-hand turn, continue straight ahead for a few metres. From the left turn, the road once again leads uphill and finally onto what Dartmoor is famous for: the open moorland. The lane is a gravel track with many gates leading off into fields either side; these fields offer snapshots of the remarkably beautiful landscape of the hills of Dartmoor. The lane goes on for roughly 1.5km and ends a few hundred metres short of the summit of Scorriton Down. Once you reach the sign for Scorriton Down Organic Farm, follow the track along to your left.

Head through two sets of gates and enjoy the excellent vantage point you are now positioned at. You will have a fantastic view of the deep valley below and its all-encompassing Scae Wood. Continue along the track downhill passing through another gate. C When you reach the bottom you will be greeted with a small wooden bridge that allows you to cross the River Mardle. The surrounding area around the bridge is an excellent place to camp for the night; it is not only beautiful, but there are a lot of trees to provide shelter from the wind.

From here, there are no signposts to guide you. Given the unpredictable nature of weather in this area, be careful as mist can quickly creep up on to you. A map, and a navigational aid, such as a GPS or compass, are essential as you will be trekking across open moorland. Although the path is very well trodden it can be hard to distinguish at the best of times. Do not rely solely on electronic devices such as phones as these can be temperamental.

From the bridge it is a long slog uphill for a considerable distance; this is possibly the most gruelling part of this section, especially if you are carrying a heavy pack. The path first bends around to the left then back around to the right. Approximately 100m up the hill, there will be a faint fork in the trail. Take the right track and continue upwards ensuring that you keep Pupers Hill summit to your right. D The track eventually becomes more defined and easier to follow. When you get to what appears to be a crossroads of sorts, head towards Hickaton Hill.

On this section, you will pass close to the remnants of another ancient settlement. You will be pleased to know that from the settlement, it is all downhill until you reach the River Avon. E At the base of the valley keep the River Avon on your left and follow it through the stone wall and gate. This area is extremely boggy and deep in places due to the amount of water running down off the surrounding hills, so bear in mind that you may need to take a slight detour up to higher ground to

Peter's Clapper Bridge

The Old Track Bed

follow the River Avon along. Head west until you see Huntingdon clapper bridge.

F Once over the bridge head straight up the hill in front of you. You will notice a zig-zag indentation in the ground that leads up to the top. It heads off slightly left then bends around to the right. Once up the top and if visibility is good you will see the elevated ruins of a building in the distance to your left. The path curves around the base of these ruins where it eventually joins up with the old track bed which used to be the Redlake Tramway.

Redlake Tramway

The old track bed used to be the Redlake Tramway. It was built to shuttle workers and supplies back and forth from Bittaford and the Red Lake China Clay Works, deep within the south plateau. You can still see a large mound over in the distance to the right. This was the location of the old clay works, there is now a large lake in its place.

You will be pleased to know all the hard work is over. You are now in the final stretch of this fantastic trail, although there is still some distance to go!
G You cannot go wrong from this point as the trail follows directly along the track bed. Although it is easy to follow, some of the low parts can become slightly flooded to ankle depth and become uncomfortable. H While passing over an old stone bridge, you will see the former ruins of the old industry. As you continue on from the bridge you will turn a corner and be greeted with the Three Barrow Tor, rising steeply above to a height of 464m. Continue south as it winds and turns around the contours of Sharp Tor and Piles Hill. Down to the right is the River Erme, it winds through and into Ivybridge. You should be able to spot more ancient settlements along the river too. Weather permitting, the views from this final stretch of the route can be quite astonishing. Looking west you can see the outskirts of Plymouth and the Plymouth Sound. You can even catch a glimpse of the Lee Moor China Clay Works.

I As you finally round Weatherdon Hill you will eventually approach a marker stone with the Two Moors Way logo engraved on it with an arrow pointing down the hill. From here, head in the direction of the arrow and straight towards the gate. This marks the entry point to Ivybridge. Head through the gate and finally leave the rugged and harsh landscape of Dartmoor behind. The county lane

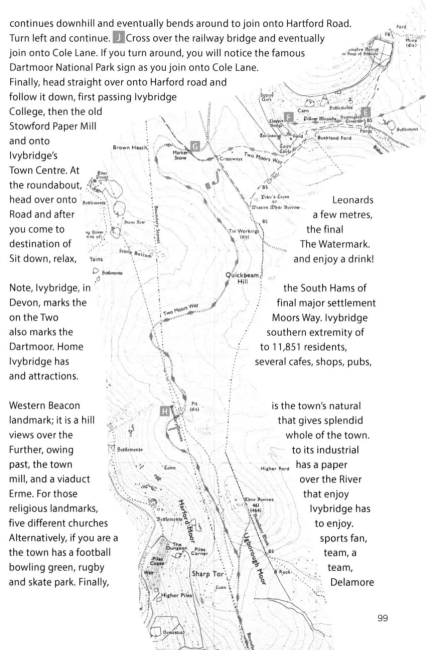

continues downhill and eventually bends around to join onto Hartford Road. Turn left and continue. [J] Cross over the railway bridge and eventually join onto Cole Lane. If you turn around, you will notice the famous Dartmoor National Park sign as you join onto Cole Lane.

Finally, head straight over onto Harford road and follow it down, first passing Ivybridge College, then the old Stowford Paper Mill and onto Ivybridge's Town Centre. At the roundabout, head over onto Leonards Road and after a few metres, you come to the final destination of The Watermark. Sit down, relax, and enjoy a drink!

Note, Ivybridge, in the South Hams of Devon, marks the final major settlement on the Two Moors Way. Ivybridge also marks the southern extremity of Dartmoor. Home to 11,851 residents, Ivybridge has several cafes, shops, pubs, and attractions.

Western Beacon is the town's natural landmark; it is a hill that gives splendid views over the whole of the town. Further, owing to its industrial past, the town has a paper mill, and a viaduct over the River Erme. For those that enjoy religious landmarks, Ivybridge has five different churches to enjoy. Alternatively, if you are a sports fan, the town has a football team, a bowling green, rugby team, and skate park. Finally, Delamore

99

Estate is just one more of the charming places you can visit in Ivybridge, and it is home to a popular art exhibition every summer. Why not celebrate the end of your walk by taking in the sights?

You deserve it!

Ivybridge Dartmoor Sign

FINISHING AT IVYBRIDGE

Ivybridge

OS Grid Ref: SX 6368 5626
District: South Hams
OS Explorer map: OL28: Dartmoor

Points of Interest

- Ivybridge Community Collage
- The Watermark (Tourist Information)
- Public Car Parks
- Ivybridge Leisure Centre
- Train Station

Accommodation and eateries

- Blanchford Hall
- The Sportsmans Inn
- Duke of Cornwall
- Imperial Inn
- Country Maid
- Friary Bakery
- Rochelle's River Café

Buses

Stagecoach, Exeter – Plymouth X38
(Mondays to Saturdays)

Stagecoach,
Ivybridge – Plymouth 20A (Mondays to
Saturdays)

Stagecoach,
Torquay – Plymouth Gold (Mondays to
Saturday)

Tavistock Country Bus,
Torquay – Tavistock (Fourth Saturday in
Month April to September)

USEFUL INFORMATION

ORGANISATIONS

Lynmouth Tourist Information
Web: www.lynton-lynmouth-tourism.co.uk
Email: world@lynton-lynmouth-tourism.co.uk
Phone: 0845 4583775

Two Moors Way Association
Web: www.twomoorsway.org
Facebook: @twomoorsway
Twitter: @twomoorsway
Email: info@twomoorsway.org

Ivybridge Tourist Information
Web: www.ivybridgewatermark.co.uk
Facebook: @Watermark.Ivybridge
Twitter: @The_Watermark
Phone: 01752 897035
Email: info@ivybridgewatermark.co.uk

Exmoor National Park
Web: www.exmoor-nationalpark.gov.uk
Facebook: @ExmoorNP
Twitter: @ExmoorNP
Email: info@exmoor-nationalpark.gov.uk
Phone: 01398 323665

Mid Devon Council
Web: www.middevon.gov.uk
Facebook: @middevon1
Twitter: @MidDevonDC
Phone: 01884 255255
Email: customerfirst@middevon.gov.uk

Dartmoor National Park
Web: www.dartmoor.gov.uk
Twitter: @dartmoornpa
Phone: 01626 832093
Email: hq@dartmoor.gov.uk

English Heritage
Web: www.english-heritage.org.uk
Facebook: @englishheritage
Twitter: @EnglishHeritage
Phone: 0370 333 1181
Email: customers@english-heritage.org.uk

Ramblers
Web: www.ramblers.org.uk
Facebook: @ramblers
Twitter: @RamblersGB
Phone: 020 7339 8500
Email: ramblers@ramblers.org.uk

Youth Hostels
Web: www.yha.org.uk
Minehead: 0800 0191 700
Email: exford@yha.org.uk
Exford 0345 371 9033
Email: minehead@yha.org.uk

COMMUNITY INFORMATION

Lynmouth
Web: www.lyntonandlynmouth.org.uk

Simonsbath
Web: www.visit-exmoor.co.uk/point-of-interest/simonsbath

Withypool
Web: www.withypoolexmoor.co.uk

Tarr Steps
Web: www.exmoor-nationalpark.gov.uk/enjoying/tarr-steps

Hawkridge
Web: www.hawkridgeexmoor.co.uk

Knowstone
Web: www.knowstone.org.uk

Witheridge
Web: www.parish.middevon.gov.uk/witheridge

Morchard Bishop
Web: www.morchardbishop-pc.org.uk

Drewsteignton
Web: www.drewsteigntonparish.co.uk

Castle Drogo
Web: www.nationaltrust.org.uk/castle-drogo

Chagford
Web: www.visitchagford.com

Widecombe-in-the-moor
Web: www.widecombe-in-the-moor.com

Holne
Web: www.visitdartmoor.co.uk/explore-dartmoor/south-dartmoor/holne

Ivybridge
Web: www.ivybridge-devon.co.uk

PUBLIC TRANSPORTATION

National Rail Enquiries
Web: www.nationalrail.co.uk
Phone: 03457 48 49 50

Filers Travel
Web: www.filers.co.uk/bus.htm
Email: info@filers.co.uk
Phone: 01271 863819

Devon Interactive Bus Map
www.cartogold.co.uk/Devon_Transport/Devon.htm

Stagecoach
Web: www.stagecoachbus.com
Email: southwest.enquiries@stagecoachbus.com
Phone: 01392 42 77 11

Dartline
Web: www.dartline-coaches.co.uk
Email: info@dartline-coaches.co.uk
Phone: 01392 872900

TAXIS

North Devon and Exmoor area

1st Call Exmoor Taxis
Phone: 07826 212511
Phone: 01643 863355

Riverside Taxis
Phone: 01598 753 442

Chris' Car
Phone: 0777 360 0125

Parkin Transfers
Phone: 07864 857806

Webbers Travel
Mini coach hire
Phone: 01598 763467

Mid Devon Area

Parkway Taxis
Phone: 01884 38899

Chulmleigh & Witheridge Taxi
Phone: 07922 131473

Loids Taxis
Phone: 07966 247253

A2B Taxis
Phone: 07971 275322

Dartmoor and South Hams Area

Dartmoor Taxis
Phone: 07854 579 973

Mooreland Taxis
Phone: 01626 835095

Finch's Taxis
Phone: 01822 890224

Ivybridge Taxis
Phone: 01752 690180

EMERGENCY SERVICES

Exmoor Search and Rescue
If an emergency, dial 999 and ask for police.
Web: www.exmoor-srt.org.uk
Facebook: @ExmoorSearchAndRescueTeam
Twitter: @ExmoorSRT
Email: info@exmoor-srt.org.uk

Dartmoor Search and Rescue
If an emergency, dial 999 and ask for police.
Web: www.dsrtashburton.org.uk
Facebook: @dartmoorrescueashburton
Twitter: @Dartmoor_SRTA
Email: info@ndsart.org.uk

NOTES:

NOTES: